THE SKY
ALONE

THE SELF ALONE

Understanding loneliness in our lives

Angela Rossmanith

CollinsDove
An imprint of HarperCollins*Publishers*

Published by Collins Dove
A division of HarperCollins*Publishers*
22–24 Joseph Street
North Blackburn Victoria 3130 Australia

First published 1995
Designed by William Hung
Cover design by William Hung
Cover illustration by Mirka Mora. Detail from *When the Soul Sleeps*, 1970,
oil paint on canvas, 61 x 51 cms. Courtesy of William Mora Galleries,
Melbourne.

Typeset by Collins Dove Typesetting
Printed by McPherson's Printing Group

The National Library of Australia
Cataloguing-in-Publication Data:

Rossmanith, Angela.
  The self alone.

  Bibliography.
  ISBN 1 86371 448 0.

  1. Loneliness. I. Title.

158.2

Acknowledgements

Our thanks go to those who have given us permission to reproduce
copyright material in this book. Particular sources of print material are
acknowledged in the text.
Every effort has been made to contact the copyright holders of text
material. The author and publisher apologise in those cases where this
has proved impossible.

Contents

Chapter three — Loneliness and us

Chapter four — Becoming lonely

Chapter five — Adolescence

Chapter eight — Relating to others

Chapter nine — Loneliness in the workplace

Chapter ten — Healing the lonely body

Thank you to my family
and friends

I fear me this — is Loneliness —
The Maker of the soul
Its Caverns and its Corridors
Illuminate — or seal —

Feeling lonely

CHAPTER 1

INTRODUCING LONELINESS

Of the great range of feelings that we humans are able to experience, loneliness is one of those that have tended to be most hidden and least admitted to publicly. We, in the Western world in particular, learn very early in life that to be lonely means to be unwanted, unpopular, friendless and flawed, and because of the fear of this cruel judgement, few of us dare to admit to loneliness or even whisper about feelings of isolation or alienation. In fact, to escape this same judgement by our own harshest critic, we might even avoid admitting those feelings to ourselves.

In a setting of trust and honesty and privacy, most people will talk of their own experiences of loneliness. To be lonely, they begin, is to have a sense of being completely and utterly alone. They look about them, but, sadly, there is no support, no outstretched hand, simply nobody there.

There is no-one to turn to during difficult times, or those moments of great joy when to share the joy expands it

1

infinitely. There is no other's heartbeat close by, and no warmth radiating from the surroundings. In the pit of the stomach, a deep hunger gnaws for something that can hardly be expressed. It is as if you are lying at the bottom of a well, alone, unable to raise anyone with your cries. It is as if you are lost and have no-one to light the way. It is feeling invisible in the middle of a crowd. It is losing all sense of meaning in life, seeing only shallowness all around. It is feeling quite sure that there is absolutely nobody out there, no God, no Great Spirit, no Guardian Angel, no Wise Person, no Eternal and Loving Mother, no Compassionate Father, no Other, no anything. It is as if you are entirely on your own, adrift and rudderless, for the term of your natural life.

That's loneliness, they say.

A subjective response

You may recognise and identify with one of these responses, or perhaps all of them. You might add some of your own, because while all feelings have their very particular distinguishing features, our experience of them is individual. My description of loneliness for myself may or may not be quite different from yours. We use our own unique expression and imagery to describe anything subtle and complex, as all feelings are.

All of us, if we are honest and self-aware, would admit to feeling lonely at times in our lives. For some, it is a haunting presence, an insistent ache that rarely eases. Attempts to quell it may only intensify the feeling, partly because the nature of the loneliness is not understood or examined closely enough. If the loneliness is a symptom of a deeper or more elusive soul-condition, then the usual prescriptions for the condition are like treating a cough with a simple lozenge when the cause is a serious infection.

For others, loneliness is a fleeting experience, a feeling that drifts by but never takes grip, a butterfly that lands briefly on the shoulder but flutters off quickly and graciously. It is something they have known, and continue to know, but it is an every-now-and-then visitor, rather than a long-term boarder.

For others again, the feeling of loneliness is something they have learned how to handle for themselves. Perhaps the wisdom that is born of years and years of experience helps to recognise it as it creeps up, to shine a gentle light on it and to welcome its gifts.

Is loneliness a modern phenomenon?

It has often been suggested that it is only our modern society that has produced loneliness. Concrete jungles, the syndrome of the latch-key kid, the demise of the nuclear family, greater individual freedom, the push for independence at all costs ... these are just some of the cited causes, or symptoms, of a decaying society which has as its consequence a population of lonely individuals.

However, there are those who disagree that loneliness is a modern syndrome, arguing that it is as old as humankind, and that we have always experienced feelings of sometimes quite extreme loneliness.[1] Take these words from the Book of Genesis: 'It is not good that man should be alone: I will make him a helpmate.' And, in the words of Aristotle: 'Without friends, no one would choose to live.'

Now in both cases there may be a number of interpretations, but we could well argue that it is the pain of loneliness that has been recognised and acknowledged. It would seem that, while the study of loneliness may be in its infancy, loneliness itself is age-old.

It was not until 1938 that what was possibly the first psychological analysis of the subject was written by Gregory Zilboorg.[2] In his article the writer made a distinction between being lonesome and being lonely. The former, he explained, is a perfectly normal and temporary state of mind which is brought on by missing somebody in particular, while loneliness, he wrote, is an experience that is both overwhelming and persistent. His distinction is debatable, being a question of semantics: song lyrics seem to use the words interchangeably.

Many behavioural scientists have turned the subject of loneliness this way and that to try to understand it and explain it and, in the case of therapists, to ease it. One such person is Robert Weiss who has been referred to as 'the father of loneliness research'[3] and who differentiated between what he called 'emotional isolation' and 'social isolation', the two faces of loneliness.

He had explanations for both as we will see, but speaking simply, what he recognised was that individuals may feel the loneliness of being isolated from others — socially isolated — or they may feel that deep emptiness that many refer to when describing their loneliness — these he would call emotionally isolated.

This is an important distinction, because it is clear that lonely feelings emerge not only when we miss other people or are left alone. In other words, there is a type of loneliness that is not explained by a sense of social abandonment or any difficulty in relating socially.

How does it feel to be lonely?
The overwhelming, persistent feeling that people refer to in describing loneliness is what is so disturbing about this loneliness business. 'All I can think about when I'm really lonely,' one person says, 'is when is it all going to end. I hate it. It's as if I'm in the grip of something bigger than I can manage.' Another adds: 'I feel empty and useless and depressed. It's hard to say whether I feel that way because I'm lonely, or whether I felt depressed first and consequently feel lonely. Whatever the case, it isn't something I like feeling.'

There is no doubt that loneliness is not a pleasant experience. True loneliness, it has been said, causes a sense of 'paralysing hopelessness and unalterable futility'.[4] Elsewhere it is referred to as 'a gnawing distress without redeeming features'.[5]

Studies have revealed that lonely people often feel anxious, tense, restless, and bored. They are also more depressed than others, although, while loneliness and depression often go hand in hand, depressed people are not always necessarily lonely, and may feel depressed for a great variety of other reasons.

Loneliness in literature and song

'"… it is so very lonely here!" Alice said in a melancholy voice; and at the thought of her loneliness two large tears came rolling down her cheeks.'[6] Alice's response reflects the sadness and sense of powerlessness that often resides in loneliness.

'I'm so lonely I could die,' cried Elvis Presley in 'Heartbreak Hotel' and he wasn't the first or last to make these feelings known in song. Huck Finn, back in the nineteenth century, had said, 'I felt so lonesome I most wished I was dead,'[7] and Holden Caulfield of *The Catcher in the Rye* said all those years later: 'I felt so lonesome, all of a sudden. I almost wished I was dead.'[8]

Mr Rochester, the blinded hero in Bronte's *Jane Eyre*, tells Jane that when she left him he '… was desolate and abandoned — my life dark, lonely, hopeless — my soul athirst and forbidden to drink — my heart famished and never to be fed.'

The Romantic poets were no less intense. Take Keats, for example:

A solitary sorrow best befits
Thy lips, and antheming a lonely grief …[9]

and Coleridge:

O Wedding-Guest! This soul hath been
Alone on a wide, wide sea;
So lonely 'twas, that God himself
Scarce seemed there to be …[10]

References to the state of loneliness abound in literature and in the lyrics of songs: its descriptions are frequent — anxious, isolated, alienated, desperate, hopeless, desolate. Lack of meaning in life and the associated loneliness are frequent themes, no doubt often reflecting the deepest concerns and personal experience of the writer.

WHAT IS LONELINESS?
The difficulty of definition

To define loneliness is as difficult as attempting to define 'sadness', or 'anger', or 'joy'. What is a feeling? Is it enough to describe the bodily sensation associated with it? Can we convert effectively into words just exactly what the experience of loneliness is?

Ask around and there is little hesitation in describing what loneliness feels like. We may all differ in our concept of loneliness, but we all seem to know whether we are lonely or not at present, or whether we have been lately. There seems to be some internal reference point that indicates a response to these questions.

A definition is rather more difficult. 'To be lonely is to be all alone in the world' is one attempt, but does not define the experience. 'Loneliness is having no-one to trust' is another.

'It is just a feeling that takes you over.'
'I am often lonely when I am with people who aren't my sort.'
'Loneliness is the weekends when everyone else is doing something and you aren't included.'
'Being lonely is being a loser, having no friends and no interests in life.'
'Loneliness is feeling you can't turn to your family because they just can't accept you.'
'Loneliness is when someone close to you dies.'
'I feel lonely when there seems no meaning, no purpose in my life.'

While these describe subjective experiences of loneliness, and while we might identify at least in part with most of them, they are not true definitions of the term, but they do give us a good idea of the range of responses that the word 'loneliness' elicits.

Social scientists, researchers, writers and philosophers have often attempted to define loneliness. Theirs are more formal statements, such as:

- 'Loneliness [is] a feeling of deprivation caused by the lack of certain kinds of human contact: the feeling that someone is missing.'[11]
- 'Loneliness ... is the exceedingly unpleasant and driving experience connected with inadequate discharge of the need for human intimacy, for interpersonal intimacy.'[12]
- 'Loneliness appears always to be a response to the absence of some particular type of relationship or, more accurately, a response to the absence of some particular relational provision.'[13]
- 'Loneliness ... is an experienced discrepancy between the kinds of interpersonal relationships the individual perceives himself [sic] as having at the time, and the kinds of relationships he would like to have, either in terms of his past experience or some ideal state that he has actually never experienced.'[14]

There are several factors that these definitions and others have in common. First of all, they agree that loneliness is the result of some kind of lack in an individual's relationships. They also agree that it is a subjective experience — in other words, we may feel lonely amongst others, or not at all lonely while we are alone. Whether or not we appear socially isolated in others' eyes may not be related at all.

Another point of agreement is that loneliness is not a pleasant feeling. Scholars in the field of loneliness differ, however, in their theoretical approaches and these differences are revealed in the varying nature of the definitions. For example, those who maintain that human needs for intimacy are paramount will reflect that in defining loneliness (see the second and third statements above), while those who stress the individual's process of perception and evaluation of their own social relationships will highlight that aspect (as the fourth statement indicates).

Academics have attacked the 'definitions' such as those formal ones quoted earlier, saying that they are mini-theories rather than definitions or even descriptions.[15]

Robert Weiss, for example, maintains that a real phenomenon, which he believes loneliness to be, can be described but not defined. To use his example, we would not try defining an elephant to someone else; we would describe it or, even better, take that person to the zoo to view it directly.

To show that loneliness was not a logical concept, which can be defined, but a real phenomenon, which can best be described, he induced the feeling of loneliness in his students by setting up a scene for them to imagine with eyes closed. He then asked them to open their eyes and jot down their feelings in that state. What resulted was a real syndrome of feelings and images, a description of something they were experiencing quite strongly.

If social scientists cannot agree on whether or not loneliness can be defined, and, even if it could be, which definition best fits it, then perhaps we should leave the subject at that. Many individuals know the feelings involved only too well, and attempts at definition can become a purely intellectual exercise that stands in the way of true understanding.

A common experience

However we regard loneliness, most of us would admit to experiencing it at some time in our lives. Echoing this theme of common experience, one writer has commented: 'Knowing no limits of class, race, or age, loneliness is ... a great leveler.'[16] It is experienced by the elite and the marginalised, the outstanding and the forgotten.

While loneliness may be common, the actual experience of it varies quite considerably across different groups and individuals in society. Those in intimate relationships would no doubt describe a different type of loneliness to the type described by those who find it difficult or even impossible to make true social contact. And the loneliness of the recently bereaved is a different loneliness to that of an adolescent in a new school and with no friends.

The meaning of loneliness varies, too, across cultures. Anthropologists report interesting observations: for example, Levy reported that the Tahitians have 'no ... terms for loneliness in the sense of being depressed or sad because of the lack of friends, companionships, and so on'.[17] Levy pointed out, though, that because these people do not have a word for loneliness does not mean that they may not express the experience in other ways. All the same, in the interviews he carried out, the loneliness theme rarely emerged.

In contrast to the Tahitians, the Eskimos have various words for the concept of loneliness. For example, in the sense of unhappiness because other people are not around they use 'hujuujaq', and to specifically refer to being or feeling left out or missing someone who has left, they use 'pai'.

In considering cultural differences, it is important to bear in mind that the language of a culture helps to define its experience. 'Language not only reflects and transmits the values and relationships of a society; it actively creates and maintains them.'[18]

In our society loneliness carries a multitude of meanings; it is a feeling that can be precipitated by a whole range of events and a feeling that can seem to arise out of nowhere. Yet we have only one word for it. Is this perhaps a reflection of our discomfort with discussing or disclosing our deepest feelings, especially when they are painful? Or is it a reflection of our difficulty in confronting and revealing loneliness in particular?

TO HIDE OR TO REVEAL?
The stigma of loneliness

Most literature based on research until now supports our suspicions that loneliness is a hidden problem. There may be a number of reasons to explain this, but it is clear that the stigma attached to the experience of loneliness is a strongly inhibiting force as far as communication is concerned.

Revealing feelings of loneliness, or any feelings for that matter, can be useful in relieving emotional tension and may well lead to closer friendships with the confidants. However, there is another less attractive possibility: revealing feelings of loneliness may also lead to negative responses and judgements that only manage to exacerbate the loneliness.

Thea is a woman in her forties, single and sometimes happy about that because of the freedom it affords, but often sad about not having a permanent relationship with what she refers to as 'a trustworthy and truly caring person'. She has a small circle of friends, but no-one she considers extremely close. She admits to frequent feelings of loneliness but says that she has learnt not to relieve the tension by telling others, even those she thinks may understand her situation quite well.

> You could say once bitten, twice shy, I suppose that's what it is. There is a stigma attached to being lonely, despite what everyone says about being more open these days. At the time of telling, other people are very sympathetic, very understanding, but afterwards you feel this curtain coming down. I could be kind and say they just don't know what to do, but I'm afraid that they are really put off by the idea of someone being lonely.

Certainly studies indicate that we have contradictory responses to others we think of as disadvantaged in some way.[19] We respond positively by showing kindness and care, by listening sympathetically, possibly by offering suggestions on how to improve the situation, but at the same time we feel unsure and awkward, perhaps not following through with our initial warmth, so that someone who was lonely may come to the conclusion that the kind and warm words may be followed by a degree of distancing.

The two sides to this are shown here: Thea's story indicates one aspect, and the following story the other.

Chris works with a young man who has approached her about his sense of isolation and loneliness, especially since a long-term relationship with a young woman ended a few months previously.

> I admire his courage in talking to someone about it, but at the same time I felt he wanted someone to do something about it, and all I did was to listen to him.
>
> I happen to think listening is very important because it helps people doing the talking to clarify things and to get it off their chest — we all need to do that at times. But in this case I felt he was disappointed I did nothing more for him, and I sense he is still waiting for some cue from me to take up the conversation, to take action, but he doesn't seem to realise that he's the only one who can really do anything much about it.

Chris's story emphasises an interesting point: what lonely people report as lack of interest or withdrawal of warmth or distancing after initial care and sympathy may be due to a misinterpretation. It would not be surprising for someone who feels they have exposed themselves by revealing their vulnerability to be ultra-sensitive to the responses of their listeners and to feel that, if their revelation is not acted upon in some positive way, they have been abandoned.

The response may, in fact, be related to the reason for the loneliness in the first place — a sense of abandonment may, for example, be part of the root cause. This is a possibility we will explore later on.

There are other possible reasons for not revealing the problem of loneliness. For example, we may feel that it is not up to others to solve our problems, or even to hear us out. We may be people who regard self-reliance highly and strive for it, even if it means being lonely for much of the time.

Then again there are those of us who believe that, even if we were to share our feeling with others, they wouldn't be able to help anyway. This is especially the case where we are feeling depressed as well as lonely and possibly in need of professional help rather than the help that the average untrained person could possibly give.

These latter people may agree with the writer of an article on loneliness back in 1959:

> People who are in the grip of severe degrees of loneliness cannot talk about it; and people who have at some time in the past had such an experience can seldom do so either, for it is so frightening and uncanny in character that they try to disassociate the memory of what it was like.[20]

Is it loneliness?

There is yet another reason for not revealing loneliness: we may not recognise that it is loneliness that we are experiencing so the subject is not an issue for discussion. This raises the obvious question: What is loneliness, then, and how does it feel?

If, as has been suggested, loneliness is a real phenomenon, then it can be described but not defined (remember the elephant story earlier), and the descriptions generally given reveal a similar pattern. It is not uncommon to recognise another person's loneliness because of our own understanding of this pattern, even when that person does not admit to feeling lonely.

Certainly some people will avoid naming their loneliness. They may refer to their condition as extreme fatigue, or dissatisfaction with their job or with their partner, confess to an ennui with life in general and an overwhelming sense of lack of meaning, yet it would seem quite clear that they are experiencing what most of us would recognise as a deep sense of loneliness.

To admit to it may elicit acute feelings of shame and guilt, because of all those negative connotations of the term. To even contemplate the admission may bring on tremblings of sheer terror. Whatever would people think? Imagine the pity, the sidelong glances, the embarrassment on their part as they struggled with knowing just what to say. Better to call it by a different name.

To avoid facing and accepting deeply painful feelings, some of us may prefer to sidestep the issue and call our experience 'loneliness' despite the taboo surrounding this very term. The feedback that we receive on reporting being lonely may be more tolerable, or even more satisfying, than if we admitted to any other feelings.

We may be viewed more sympathetically and treated more tenderly by relatives or friends or acquaintances. We may feel it lends a mystique to us as we identify, in our daydreams, with tragic heroines and heroes who felt misunderstood, shunned by society and consequently lonely.

We may associate loneliness with genius, or superior creative powers, and because we rather like seeing ourselves, and being seen, in that light, we report deep and inconsolable loneliness. We may simply not be aware of anything beyond the darkness, and 'feeling lonely' is as close as we can come to identifying what it is that taunts us.

Revealing loneliness

Despite loneliness being largely a hidden problem, there are circumstances under which we will actually reveal how we feel. It seems, for example, that we are more likely to talk about being lonely when we are first aware of the feeling than further down the track when the sense of isolation may well be entrenched.

The perceived cause of the loneliness is another factor in whether or not we reveal loneliness. In general, it would seem that if we regard external circumstances to be the cause then we are more likely to reveal it because others will not judge us so badly: to lose one's partner, for example, is generally regarded as sad and leading to feelings of loneliness in the bereaved partner. Relocation by a company or being left by a spouse are other external circumstances that we see as understandable reasons for loneliness.

Being unable to get along with other people, on the other hand, is not in the same category. If we see ourselves as being unpopular, if our self-concept is poor and our self-esteem is low, then our loneliness can be a source of shame for us. This is seen quite clearly as an internal cause of our loneliness, and because we have great fears of being judged, then we are most unlikely to admit to feeling lonely.

It is not altogether surprising to find that females are more likely to reveal their loneliness than are males and that society regards a lonely female in a more kindly light than a lonely male.[21] Why might this be?

Perhaps it is because females are more likely to communicate their emotional state than males that it is less surprising if they reveal their feelings of loneliness, and perhaps because we continue to be culturally conditioned to expect men not to reveal vulnerabilities, however much we demand that they be sensitive and open.

Further on the research front, other results tell us that it is extroverted and social individuals who are more likely to confide details about themselves[22] and that chronically lonely people tend not to be outgoing and find socialising difficult.[23] The combined results lead us to conclude that the lonely tend not to confide in others, at least as far as personal details go. Some aspects of the stereotyped image of the lonely individual are here supported: socially shy and unable to talk with any degree of intimacy.

It would seem natural that self-disclosure is most likely to occur with those with whom we are intimate. Some studies substantiate this belief: for example, one study of widows and how they cope with their loneliness revealed that most of them turned to friends, children or siblings for help rather than the helping professionals.

On the other hand, we often turn to complete strangers to pour out our hearts. In fact, we may share with strangers what we would never dream of sharing with a friend. Why? It would seem obvious that it happens because we assume we will never see these strangers again, and that they are highly unlikely to know anyone that we know.

But is this tendency — to confide in total strangers — a sign of something more fundamental? Does the confiding have much substance or do we reel off scripts that provide lines that allow us to 'make contact' without making real contact?

Self-disclosure — help or hindrance?

In our culture's push for honesty and openness and emotional vulnerability in relationships, a new phenomenon has emerged gradually: the use of self-disclosure as a way of engaging others.

An emphasis on openness has tended to become a guiding principle, with therapists and counsellors advising open communication as the key to relationship success and conflict resolution. And, for deepening intimacy, at least some degree of openness is certainly essential. However, to what extent is self-disclosure regarded as 'a marketable commodity'?[24] In a culture that is increasingly stressing the desirability of being psychologically aware and expressing feelings, the conclusion might be drawn that to openly display these characteristics would mean being more attractive to others.

Hand-in-hand with this approach is the emphasis on instancy: instant food, instant drink, instant entertainment. Why not instant intimacy?

Kerry's story tells of just this.

It's happened twice now, where within twenty-four hours of meeting a man I've told him as much as I can possibly imagine about myself. You know the sort of thing —

family history, personal hang-ups, problems with past relationships, what I'm working through at the moment. Can you imagine? No wonder they took off as soon as possible.

Looking back now, I see that I wanted them to think I was fascinating and to like me instantly. I know all about good relationships needing to develop at their own pace, and revealing appropriately, but when you have someone in front of you and you want to make an impression then being your boring old self just doesn't seem good enough.

The need that Kerry mentions, to appear fascinating and to be liked, underpins this approach — self-disclosure serves as a hook to capture and captivate the listener. Research does indicate that a high degree of self-disclosing early on in a relationship can lead to intense attraction, but it does not do much for a sense of trust.[25] Perhaps that is because a person who reveals all in one sitting may be seen as lacking discretion and any sense of privacy.

'The worst part,' Kerry continues, 'is that I felt as if I were going through the motions and not really relating at all, even though I was reeling off all these personal details.' And herein lies the problem of using self-disclosure to sell ourselves: going through the motions is quite a different matter from being genuinely connected, and all it can do is intensify the deep sense of isolation that led to the self-disclosing in the first place. While Kerry continues to refer to her 'boring old self', she is denying her own richness and the potentialities she holds, as well as alienating herself from her own true self. Now, this is true loneliness.

PERCEIVING AND LABELLING LONELINESS
The subjective perspective

The way we see things — our perceptions — goes towards defining an experience for us. This is because we interpret what happens against a backdrop of our beliefs and our past experiences. It is as if we unconsciously and spontaneously check with these whenever we interact with other people and whenever we are faced with a situation, whatever it may be.

Let's say there is a discrepancy between how we relate socially and how we would like to relate socially. For example, let's say that you believe that the average sociable person — like yourself — should have social contact every weekend at least a couple of times, and perhaps once or twice during the week. Otherwise, you believe, you would feel terribly lonely. If you are no longer experiencing the level of social contact you believe to be acceptable, then it is likely that you feel lonely.

If, on the other hand, I am quite happy with some social contact once every couple of months, then I would feel happier than you do, and less lonely, even though you have social contact a couple of times a week: the reason is that you would expect more to satisfy your needs for frequent interaction.

It seems that each of us has an optimal level of social interaction — a level with which we feel comfortable — and we may experience loneliness when the social relations fall below this level. We know they fall because our past experience and that of other people around us provide a yardstick for comparison.

The nature of the distress we experience because of the loneliness depends on various factors: individuals interpret and react to loneliness in many ways, so the response may involve feelings of anxiety, anger, bitterness or sadness, or it might surface in behaviour such as drug or alcohol abuse and what are termed 'eating disorders'.

Our reaction depends a lot on what we believe are our reasons for being lonely. If we blame others — for leaving us, for example, or for giving us false hope, or for not providing a safe environment when we were growing up — then we are likely to feel angry and bitter.

However, if we believe that we ourselves are responsible for the condition — perhaps because we are not fascinating or

interesting enough or because we've offended other people —
then we would be more likely to feel sad and depressed.

What is interesting here is that we can actually change
feelings of sadness and depression to feelings of anger and
bitterness by changing the way we view the reason for being
lonely, but we would not actually diminish the loneliness
itself.

With all these different emotions bubbling away, how do
we know that the feeling of loneliness is among them? There
are a number of elements involved here: emotional patterns
and behavioural patterns allow us to recognise that it is
loneliness that we are experiencing. In terms of behavioural
cues, we might be enjoying less social contact than we once
did, and even when we interact with other people, the
interactions might be more and more unsatisfying. Emotional
cues include a cluster of feelings revolving around
unhappiness. Obviously, feeling unhappy, sad, depressed or
frustrated will not on its own define the experience of
loneliness — the perception of loneliness requires more.

When loneliness is considered to be the frequent result of
a discrepancy between our social life and how we would
desire it to be, there is a subjective perspective involved, and
so what outsiders perceive and how they would assess the
situation are not relevant. All that matters is how we ourselves
perceive our own situation and whether or not it measures up
to what we feel is a satisfying pattern of relating.

While two of us might seem to have the same sorts of
patterns, we may perceive our own situations quite differently,
so that one of us feels quite desolately lonely and the other
feels content and fulfilled. Sometimes we see this discrepancy
in a couple. Jane and Mark, who have been together for ten
years, have tried to come to terms with this problem.

> Jane likes frequent contact with people, while I am quite
> happy to have quiet weekends, away from people. When
> we do close the doors for a quiet time, Jane becomes

restless, and has even been very upset sometimes, because she says she feels lonely and isolated when she has so little outside contact.

Even though she sees more people during the week, she still likes lots of contact on the weekend too, and that's awful for me. We've had to reach some compromises — sometimes I just go away for the weekend to a friend's mountain house so that she can have people in, sometimes she just accepts that it will be a people-free weekend, and sometimes I just accept that a few people will be dropping by.

Mark's love of solitude clashes with Jane's heightened sociability, but they have tried to meet the differences with compromise.

Personal standards

How do we arrive at standards for our own social relations? How do we assess whether we have enough friends, whether we interact sufficiently, whether the relationships we do have are satisfying enough?

A lonely person may well make comments such as: 'I don't have any friends', or 'I can't seem to communicate with anyone', or 'I'm not outgoing like other people, I can't make friends'. These statements, poignant as they are, reflect an implicit standard.

We arrive at our standards in a couple of ways. One is by using past experience as a reference point, by gradually building an idea of what leads us to feel satisfied and learning how to meet our needs in a social context. Various studies emphasise the importance of these standards, showing that when people feel lonely and dissatisfied it is associated with their perception that things used to be better than they are now.

Notice the word 'perception': the implication is that things may not actually have been better, but they are being perceived that way. People who indulge in nostalgia tend to think along these lines — it certainly provides a sort of safety net, musing on the 'good old days'. But while we are dwelling on them, we are forgetting about making the present and the future enjoyable times, too.

However independent we may feel and however much we profess not to be influenced by those around us, we do compare our own social relations with those of others and evaluate our own position accordingly. Others may seem to have more social contact and to derive great satisfaction from that, so we may conclude that our social contact is impoverished by comparison.

For young people especially, the images that the media thrusts at them may be particularly unsettling: vital, laughing, carefree young people gather in partying groups, enjoying life, the sun and the sand. However sophisticated and detached the observer, the message is clear: here are people having a very good time with no difficulties in relating or attracting. So what's wrong with me? asks the young person curled up on the couch, alone, with perhaps no social event coming up in the near future.

It isn't just young people who are susceptible to media images and their messages. How many adults would admit honestly to feeling more than just a little inadequate in light of the good life that is the reward for looking this way or that, for having this or that talent, for using just the right product? These images can become stamped on our psyches, and we need to apply great strength of will and great strength of purpose to recognise them for what they are.

Our own standards for social relations may change over time. We may, for example, rearrange our priorities as we become older, putting less effort and energy into work and more into the cultivation of friendships and companionship. The proliferation of personal development and growth courses has raised the consciousness of many who have subsequently reassessed their relationships and their priorities.

Unfortunately, standards may change in a different way. Very lonely people may change their standards to fit what they now regard as grim reality, shrinking their psyches to match an already narrowing world. 'Can't make friends? Don't need them anyway. I'm not trying anymore,' is their cry.

CHAPTER 2

Understanding loneliness

SOME APPROACHES

If we are to understand the phenomenon of loneliness it would be useful for us to explore a couple of issues. First of all, what is the nature of loneliness — for example, is it a normal condition, or an abnormal one? Can it be a positive experience, or is it of necessity always a negative experience?

Secondly, what causes loneliness? Do the causes arise from within the individual or do they live within the environment? Is it something within me, within my history and my life experience, that causes me to feel lonely? Or is it out there in the world around me, in the society of which I am a part?

Let's consider each of these issues and how they might be related. There are three main schools of thought regarding the causes of loneliness, seen as:

- the result of early experiences, or
- the result of the interplay between individual and society, or
- part of the human condition.

Early experiences

The first approach, which we will discuss in more detail in Chapter Four, has it that the experience of loneliness is largely and perhaps even entirely the result of early influences, that is, particular experiences in infancy and childhood. This idea is based on Freudian concepts, and while Freud himself did not explore loneliness in his research or his writings, those who followed in his footsteps have done so.

Although psychologists in this tradition see the seeds of loneliness in childhood, they differ in their beliefs as to how it arises. For example, according to one writer the lonely person 'seldom fails to display an ill-disguised or open hatred'[1] directed either inwardly or else towards other people, and stemming from the infantile experience of omnipotence.

The origins of this attitude, part of the egocentricity of the lonely, he wrote, begin early, when the baby is loved and admired on the one hand, but is dependent on others to gratify needs on the other hand. Here was the root of later narcissism and even megalomania, he maintained. It would seem that he saw loneliness in very negative terms.

Others have talked of a deficit in social skills as being due to poor interaction between parents and children,[2] this deficit, together with the strong drive for human intimacy — the need to be close to at least one other human being — leading to feelings of loneliness. And one writer[3] deplored the 'premature weaning from mothering tenderness' which she saw as leading to the development of the lonely personality.

Later on we will consider the importance of attachment theory in explaining the experience of loneliness. This theory is based on the work of John Bowlby, a leading researcher in the field of mother–child relationships, who has pointed out that at particular times in our lives we tend to bond strongly with certain other individuals. While these bonds are sure and strong we feel secure, whereas if the bonds are broken we experience anxiety and distress. If the bonds are broken in infancy or childhood, there is a response pattern that seems very close in style and intensity to the loneliness that individuals report in adulthood.

Many of those who believe that loneliness has its roots in childhood experience have been clinicians whose patients often present with deep and complex problems of which loneliness is just one aspect. It is not surprising, then, that for them loneliness tends to be an unhealthy experience or even an abnormal condition.

Others believe that there is no perfect early experience, that we all carry scars into adulthood and, depending on our environment and the choices we make, feelings of loneliness may or may not be a large part of our lives as a result.

Society and us

Not everyone believes that early experience plays such a large part in our lives. Some put more emphasis on the relationship between society and the individual in attempting to understand the causes of loneliness.

Let's look at it from their point of view. To live happily in society — which is to say to be part of the group — we may feel pressured to behave in socially approved ways. We have this experience quite early in life: the socialisation process begins from the time we begin to explore our environment. We are taught good manners, we start to learn from trial and error what wins other people over and what might lead them to reject us (although some of us take longer than others to learn).

The process can become a burden if we allow our social roles — the way we behave towards others in a social setting — to define who we are. The roles are often limiting and repressive, and so there can arise a discrepancy between who we really are and who we show to the world. Caught up in playing socially acceptable roles, we lead empty, meaningless lives. Even if we don't engage entirely in such roles ourselves, we may be affected by those who do. Loneliness may be a consequence of a perceived discrepancy between the degree

of social contact we would like to have and the actual extent
of it.

How do we establish our social standards? By looking at
those around us. Conditioned by the cultural stereotype of
'more is better' (more friends, more contacts, more social
activity) we might like our lives to be as exciting as we
imagine others' to be.

We may decide not to go along with society and its
demands, to turn our backs on the cultural stereotypes, to
drop our defences, to be more honest about ourselves and
therefore more vulnerable. In doing so, we may have the
expectation of being rejected by other people who sit in
judgement and so feel ourselves to be social outcasts.

One writer puts it like this:

> Loneliness … is sharpest and most poignant in the
> individual who has, for one reason or another, found
> himself [sic] standing, without some of his customary
> defences, a vulnerable, frightened, lonely but real self,
> sure of rejection in a judgmental world.[4]

Trapped behind a variety of social roles, we can come to
feel that our real selves are not acceptable or lovable; it is this
perception that 'keeps people locked in their loneliness'.[5] The
discrepancy between our actual selves — what we refer to
elsewhere as our authentic selves — and our idealised selves, the
way we feel we should be as defined by society, can cause
inconsolable feelings of loneliness because of the alienation
between the me that I know and the me that I present to the
world.

Those caught up in this process have been described as
'other-directed'.[6] Other-directed people want to be liked, and
so they conform, checking their behaviour constantly to ensure
that they are following ground rules. The other-directed
individual is distanced from feelings and the inner self, and the
need to conform results in a constant anxiety and a great need
to be popular with peers, a hunger that is rarely satisfied.

There is another point of view to be considered here. What if the problem lies not in being 'other-directed' but in being 'me-directed'? We may want to be part of community, to be engaged in meaningful activity with the rest of the group, but there is pressure to stand on our own, to be independent of all others and to tread our own path. Individualism, one writer has said, is based on the attempt to ignore the fact that humans are interdependent. One of the main goals of technology, he believes, is 'to "free" us from the necessity of relating to, submitting to, depending upon, or controlling other people. Unfortunately, the more we have succeeded in doing this, the more we have felt disconnected, bored, [and] lonely.'[7] We will examine the idea of individualism and how it relates to loneliness more closely later on.

Whether we decide to base our behaviour on what we feel others want or whether we decide to stand alone and apart, individuals to the last, we are still involved in trying to meet some basic needs. And in both cases we are conforming to what we perceive as a social ideal. While for some it is the friendly, helpful person who falls in with others to the detriment of their own inner self, for others it is the independent individual who is admired for such self-reliance. Whatever the case, according to this school of thought it is the interplay between individual and society that leads to the common experience of loneliness.

The human condition

Loneliness may be the result of early experiences, and it may be the result of social forces acting on the individual, but it may also be 'part of the human condition' — just a part of being a human with the full range of emotions and responses that are ours.

Believing that human beings are fundamentally alone and that loneliness is just a fact of life, existentialists, as they are known, put their emphasis on how to deal with loneliness rather than on what causes it.

One of the main writers in this tradition, Clark Moustakas,[8] has made a distinction between true loneliness and loneliness anxiety. The latter, he explains, is a motivating force in seeking constant activity with other people. Anxious about feeling lonely and about how others will view us if we are seen alone, we engage in a frenzy of relating with others, superficially or otherwise, to avoid the pain and humiliation of loneliness. Here are social forces at work once again.

As for true loneliness, he writes, each true experience of it 'involves a confrontation or an encounter with oneself'.[9] While the confrontation can cause chaos, throwing us into turbulence and pushing us towards using energies and resources we may never have used before in order to come to terms with our life, encounter 'is a joyous experience of self-discovery'. Both, Moustakas writes, are 'ways of advancing life and coming alive ... they are ways of breaking out of the uniform cycles of behaviour ...'[10]

A conglomerate view

Could it be that there are different types of loneliness, each of which might have its roots in different places? There may be a loneliness that arises from early experience of separation or breaking of close bonds; there may be a loneliness that comes from how we relate to those around us and how we perceive ourselves, and perhaps how we should be in the social context; and there may be a loneliness that is as much a part of us as is any emotion — whether we choose to express it may depend on our situation, our experience of life and our outlook. As we discussed in Chapter One, we may call our essential loneliness by another name, or we may simply refrain from revealing it at all.

I would like to accept that all of the possible causes of loneliness that we've considered here are valid: some of us may relate to them all, some of us to none, but I would guess that the majority of people would recognise the roots of their own loneliness somewhere amongst them.

TYPES OF LONELINESS

Can the loneliness a widow feels be the same sort of loneliness as that of a person who would like a more active social life? Can the loneliness of a shy, retiring individual who finds it too difficult to reach out to others be compared in any way to the loneliness of the person who reaches the mid-life point, feels dissatisfied and questions the meaning of their life?

My instinctive response to such questions is this: that there is a cluster of emotions related to feelings of loneliness — amongst them sadness, a sense of loss and possibly grief, emptiness, meaninglessness, fear, apprehension — and depending on the event (or non-event) that triggers the lonely feelings, different emotions will come into play.

The essence of loneliness, then, may not vary but different aspects of it are experienced in different situations and at different times. Let's see what thoughts about types of loneliness have emerged from various discussions.

A philosophical tradition

Philosophers have busied themselves with questions about the phenomenon of loneliness, and shown great interest in those aspects of solitude and loneliness that are either positive or negative. They have written of the benefits of aloneness, the opportunities solitude provides for deep reflection and better understanding, and for communication with one's God and with one's self.

What emerges regularly from some philosophical discussions is that the experience of solitude as a positive thing is the authentic or true form, whereas the negative experience of loneliness is a pathological variation on the theme.

Other philosophers have distinguished between that loneliness that is part of the human condition — existential loneliness — and loneliness as a reaction to lack of relationships or loss of them — psychological loneliness. Mijuskovic,[11] for example, says: 'I am not maintaining that we feel or think we are alone all the time and at every moment.

I am convinced that we really are, but are not always conscious of it.'

Along the same lines, a distinction has been made between 'primary' loneliness, which is the result of being aware of aloneness in the world, and 'secondary' loneliness, the consequence of the loss of a close other, or a deficit in social relationships.

Although researchers in the field of loneliness have acknowledged existential/primary loneliness as a very possible phenomenon, it is the psychological/secondary loneliness that has been the subject of most questioning and probing.

Isolation — emotional and social

In broad terms, the distinction between the loneliness of emotional isolation and the loneliness of social isolation makes good sense. These states were first named by Robert Weiss in his landmark publication on the subject in 1973.[12] He explained emotional isolation as resulting from the absence of an attachment figure, and social isolation by the absence of a satisfying social network. Note the use of 'absence' rather than 'loss', which has as its main consequence grief rather than loneliness.

The idea of attachment is an interesting one, based as it is in infancy and childhood and, in Weiss's view, undergoing some modification until, in adulthood, parents are replaced as attachment figures.

The absence of a close emotional attachment results in the loneliness of emotional isolation, Weiss wrote, and the only cure is a new emotional attachment, or else a reintegration of the lost attachment. 'Those experiencing this form of loneliness are apt to experience a sense of utter aloneness, whether or not the companionship of others is in fact accessible to them.'[13]

Lonely people, according to Weiss, may describe the world around them as 'desolate, barren or devoid of others', or they may express their sense of aloneness in terms of 'an empty inner world', in which case they may say they feel empty, dead inside, or hollow.

The loneliness of social isolation, on the other hand, has to do with the lack of a social network that involves us, and, Weiss wrote, can be remedied only by accessing such a network. 'The dominant symptoms of this form of loneliness are feelings of boredom or aimlessness, together with feelings of marginality.'[14]

A variety of relationships can address the loneliness of social isolation. It has been shown that friendships, family ties and work relationships can supply the social contact we need to avoid a sense of social isolation. The extent to which any one of these 'communities' can satisfy us depends on our age and stage of life; for example for some people facing a difficult time in their lives, kinship connections may be all that they require and respond to, while for others friends fill that need very well. Others again may find that the rather more impersonal and less intense nature of work relationships is more helpful to them at that time.

The distinction between the two types of isolation as defined by Robert Weiss has not always been corroborated, however. In a Dutch study,[15] which was expected to distinguish emotionally lonely people from the socially lonely, all the types of loneliness observed seemed to be forms of emotional loneliness.

Rather than abandon the concept of the loneliness of social isolation because of such results, however, researchers continue to ask questions and to work at uncovering the underlying dynamics of loneliness, whatever its antecedents.

Loneliness — chronic or short-term?

When we are considering types of loneliness it is important to examine the emotional aspects involved — what feelings in particular are present or absent? We need to consider, too, the sorts of deprivation people experience — what relationships are essential to an individual (and it goes without saying that this varies widely from person to person) and which ones are missing?

There is a further dimension that has been recognised, however: how long does the loneliness last, and for how long does a lonely person anticipate it will last? Three types of loneliness may be distinguished on the basis of a time perspective.

- Transient loneliness is self-explanatory — it is a fleeting experience, visiting only briefly.
- Situational loneliness occurs as the result of a crisis such as death or separation, or a change such as leaving home or having children leave home.
- Chronic loneliness is a long-term experience, reflecting an inability to develop social relations that are satisfying in any appreciable way. Attitudes and beliefs of the chronically lonely — those who have felt lonely for more than two years or so — tend to be firmly entrenched.

The importance of distinguishing between time spans where loneliness is concerned lies in the fact that, while two individuals may describe identical feelings of loneliness, the reasons for one who has been feeling this way for four weeks since she separated from a partner, for example, would be entirely different from those of another who has been feeling this way for a couple of years.

The understanding of this very difference is essential to the understanding of loneliness and the ways to alleviate it.

PERSONALITY AND LONELINESS
The lonely type

Is there a type of person who is more vulnerable to loneliness than others might be? In considering whether or not we can answer this question it is interesting to note that different people describing themselves as lonely may mean entirely different things, and so we need an 'average idea' of what feeling lonely means to these different people. One person may mean that it is difficult to make contact in a social situation, another may mean that maintaining relationships with others is an impossibility, another may be experiencing feelings of low self-esteem and yet another may be feeling out of touch with the Universe and have lost any sense of real meaning in life.

As these examples illustrate, the range of meanings can be vast, and so trying to describe a 'typical lonely person' is not within our domain. However, some researchers[16] have come up with a list of major features that represents the prototype of the lonely person — the prototype refers to a composite of the most common characteristics of a lonely individual. This points to the fact that it is a cluster of feelings and behaviours and thoughts by which we identify loneliness, and not by one particular defining feature.

Based on subjects' descriptions of a lonely person, the most commonly occurring features were tabulated. These included 'avoids social contact and isolates self from others', 'feels depressed', 'thinks "I want a friend"'. The feelings mentioned were those of an interpersonal type: rejected, angry, isolated, inferior.

Results indicated that the characteristics of the lonely person can be grouped into three main categories:

- The largest category refers to thoughts and feelings of being apart from other people, of feeling isolated and different, unloved and inferior to others.
- The second set involves the sorts of actions that result in loneliness: the avoidance of social contacts, isolating oneself from other people.
- The third set includes feelings of paranoia, of feeling angry and depressed.

Further research by the same people has revealed that lonely people have more problems that relate to socialising than do non-lonely people. The most common problem to emerge was contained in the statement: 'I find it hard to make friends in a simple, natural way.' Furthermore, they tend to attribute their failures in the interpersonal arena to a lack of ability, but they don't put their successes down to any ability on their part. In fact, because they attribute their loneliness to character faults in themselves they tend to feel, too, that there is little if any hope for change, believing that they are who they are and their character is impossible to change.

Non-lonely types of people put failures down to prevailing conditions: they believe that next time they will try harder, or try a different method. But because very lonely people see themselves as incompetent they start feeling quite soon that they may as well stop trying. If they can, they begin avoiding interpersonal situations, leading to fewer chances to develop social skills, which leads to more socialising disaster and so on, leading eventually to complete social withdrawal. And so it is that the deeply lonely person is drawn into a negative spiral that has total isolation as its core.

Dimensions of loneliness

In one survey[17] in which several hundred people were interviewed quite extensively, various loneliness measures were included together with questions concerning background characteristics, social contacts, measures of self-esteem and measures of depression.

There was roughly the same number of men and women and they were single, married, divorced and widowed. The results revealed four quite distinct types. The largest group of these was not lonely or else only slightly lonely, while the other groups showed varieties of types of loneliness. Compared to the others, the non-lonely appeared to enjoy a fairly large network of varying relationships. They also seemed to have a number of close relationships and were happy with them.

On the other hand, another group expressed strong feelings of dissatisfaction with their relationships; they did not have a close partner and felt empty and abandoned. A large percentage of divorced men and women fell into this category. The main motifs were lack of intimate relationships, feeling socially deprived and feeling that the future was hopeless.

Yet another group had a few intimate relationships although they did not have a spouse or other main attachment figure. This type was made up of more never-married men and women than the other types, and they tended to see their loneliness as temporary only.

The last group, made up mainly of widowed men and women who were mostly over fifty-five years old and many of whom were unemployed, seemed to accept their situation as unavoidable. They did not feel abandoned by others, nor did they blame others for the state they were in. However, they did tend to feel that their loneliness was a permanent state; to use the researchers' own terminology, they had 'an endless time perspective' where loneliness was concerned.

In summary, what this study revealed was that there are dimensions to loneliness — time perspective is one, and the nature of missing relationships is another — and that the experience usually varies across the population. Married people, for example, showed up as least likely to feel lonely, and for lonely individuals feelings of despair were more common among the divorced and widowed than among those who had never married.

While results such as these offer interesting insights into vulnerabilities to loneliness, we need to take great care in our interpretation of them. Obviously there are many divorced people who are far happier and healthier than ever they were when they were with their partners, and there are many widowed individuals who have managed to find meaning and fulfilment in their lives despite the loss of a partner.

All the same, what the results do imply is that having had a relationship, and especially one that has provided at least a degree of companionship, the absence or loss of significant others in our lives can set us up for the experience of loneliness. The breadth of our social networks and the existence for us of other intimates can, however, mitigate this experience.

Needs for privacy

The extent to which any one of us enjoys or seeks social interaction varies widely. While some of us are naturally gregarious and outgoing, rating interpersonal connections as a very high priority in our lives, others of us are private people, content with our own company more often than not.

How the privacy manifests itself may differ from person to person: one may be very private about his 'love life', while another may never speak about her position at work. Another may enjoy a hobby without telling many others about it, and still another person may be private about their family of origin. There are those individuals, too, who share very little about any aspect of their lives, the very truly private people who keep very much to themselves.

There are good reasons to keep some things private. Let's consider some personal examples.

Joe talks to no-one but his girlfriend Kristen (and to her very little) about his childhood and his family of origin.

> It isn't as if it was traumatic, but it just doesn't seem relevant at the moment to talk about it. Kristen complains and says she'd understand me better if she knew more about my growing up years, and I've joked to her that maybe I don't want her to know me better! It might be my way of being a bit independent, having this part of my life that is just mine and no-one else's.

Sandra talks to no-one of her hobby. Her friends know that she makes the little dolls she works on so meticulously, stitching on tiny button-eyes and braiding tufts of golden and dark brown wool for hair.

> I am passionate about my dolls, and each of them has a personality of her own. I give most of them away to hospitals and to friends and their kids, but I don't talk about this hobby — this mad obsession of mine. When I was small I had lots and lots of dolls, mostly handmade, and I get so much enjoyment out of making them now. I

live alone, but I never feel alone because of them — and my friends, of course!

Neither Joe nor Sandra has a chronic loneliness problem: both have others with whom to share their lives, even though they do keep an aspect to themselves. Joe explains this by admitting that perhaps he would like not to be understood any better than he is already; he may, in time, feel differently and decide to divulge some details of his early life. For now, though, he prefers to maintain some privacy.

Sandra's doll-making is a creative expression of herself that she does not feel compelled to talk about. It satisfies a need in her that requires no other form of communication than the very making of these little things.

Those for whom all their lives must remain private are in a different category from Joe and Sandra. They are not necessarily the solitaries of our society, although they do tend to be. They are not keen to seek out company but prefer their own, and for them communication is a chore rather than an ideal.

Any loneliness they experience has more to do with shyness and difficulty in reaching out to others than with any decision to live alone: they enjoy solitude more than most, although there are times in their lives when they may feel intolerably alone. They may console themselves with the idea that the loneliness they feel in being alone is preferable to the burden of living and being with others day after day, hour after hour.

Paradoxically, lack of privacy can lead to desperate loneliness. The reason lies in the fact that keeping private certain areas of our lives serves to preserve our integrity. If I hug something to myself — whether it is past experience, or a hobby, or my work — then I regard it as part of me, and to part with it may lead to a feeling of having lost oneself somehow. An invasion of privacy can be a devastating theft, robbing an individual as it can of their sense of self.

We must protect our selves from such invasion, not by becoming secretive and holding back when it is more appropriate to give forth, but by taking time to strengthen the self (more about the importance of the self in the next chapter).

Loneliness and us

3

BECOMING AN INDIVIDUAL

There are different ways of viewing loneliness and different types of loneliness. But who is it that is feeling the loneliness? Who is the 'self' that is alone and lonely? Why are some of us affected by one type of loneliness and perhaps not another?

Becoming an individual requires us to see ourselves as separate from others, and to develop a self-concept that is based on our interactions with others. Now we will look at how the process comes about.

Our life's goal

A baby is born, and the event is cause for celebration. A newborn is invariably a reminder for us of new life, new hope, and a tomorrow. What happens, though, between the time that we hold this tiny person who is so dependent on others for survival, and the time that this person becomes a young adult with particular values and interests, beliefs and attitudes?

How does each of us develop a 'self', the unique individual that is each of us? Our 'core', as it has sometimes been called?

Our individuality, as Durkheim referred to it? Carl Jung wrote: 'The self is our life's goal for it is the completest expression of that fateful combination we call individuality.'[1] How then do we start on this 'life's goal'?

Each individual has a unique biological structure, but this is not enough to build a self. It cannot be built in a vacuum. What is required is a social environment, because it is only through continuous interchange between an individual and other people that a self can develop. In fact, back in 1902, sociologist Charles Cooley[2] suggested that our concept of our self evolves from social interactions and will go through a number of changes over the course of our life. He used the term the 'looking-glass self' to refer to the fact that our identity is a reflection of other people's reactions to us.

While most people agree that infants are born without a sense of self, there is no such agreement on just when they begin to become self-aware, although many contemporary theorists believe that the first signs appear between four and six months of age.

The minimal social environment for a child is itself with mother who is the first point of contact. Her interactions with her infant — when she gazes into the eyes, when she strokes the tiny body, when she coos and smiles at the child, when she makes encouraging noises in response to the infant's movements — these are the foundations for its sense of self. Loved and accepted, encouraged and nurtured, he/she grows in an environment that supports him or her as a human being.

Most babies have much more than minimal social contact. They have a father, possibly siblings, grandparents, relatives, friends. All their interactions with the child go to make up its experience, and a unique experience it is. It is accumulated experience that goes to make the 'self'.

A healthy self
A healthy self is not much different from a healthy body which needs nourishing food to flourish. The food for the self

though, is the perceptive process, which means that process of seeing our world and what happens in it.

But consider how much is going on around us at any time: consider the energies of other people, how they are relating to us, the situations that are taking place, the tiny little bits and pieces that make up the rich life we see out there. The fact is that we can't possibly take that much in, and what happens is that we choose what we perceive.

How do we make our choices? By keeping to what we have experience in, and by choosing that which would seem to enhance the self, rather than endanger or damage it. This is especially true during the early years of life, when the self is first developing.

While a baby has the potential for a healthy self, whether or not it develops in a healthy manner depends very much on the experience with other people. In this way, the quality of the relationships with others influences the growth of the self.

Whatever the experiences we have, whatever the perceptions we choose, we need some protection for the times when the environment is dangerous — such as when we have interactions with others whose self is unhealthy or crippled. We develop, for this purpose, a screen that protects, but if we are subjected to an unhealthy environment over a period of time, the screen becomes thicker and more rigid, so that eventually nothing at all is let in. The consequence is that our self has a barrier around it, and becomes a prisoner of itself engaging in no communication and closed off to all others.

It is in this situation that the self becomes malnourished, missing out as it does on the food that others' interactions provide. And it is in this situation that the self becomes isolated, alienated and lonely. This is not to say that the situation cannot be reversed: the barriers can come down, even imperceptibly at first, if a person chooses to engage in positive relationships. These involve exchanging ideas with others, receiving feedback from others and being involved with others — and are at the heart of individual growth.

Self and self-concept

Let's consider again what Jung wrote: 'The self is our life's goal ...' The implication here is that the self is what we work towards developing to its full potential. It is our life experience and our interactions with other people that help to illuminate who we really are. They act as mirrors, reflecting what we cannot otherwise see.

We may not be born with a sense of self, but we do have particular attributes that make us unique individuals, and as we interact with others we become more aware of these attributes. However, our awareness of the attributes goes towards forming our self-concept, while the attributes themselves are part of who we are.

Saying that our attributes are part of who we are raises some tricky questions: are we born with certain traits? In other words, is part of personality innate? Or do we arrive in the world as clean slates, ready and willing to be written on?

The general consensus is that we are born with potential for certain ways of behaving and that our environment interacts to shape us to some extent. Data from several studies imply that a few components of human temperament can be inherited, such as activity level and irritability. It has been suggested, too, that most infants show a pattern of temperamental characteristics that can have some influence over the child's reaction to various situations later in life, although these patterns can be modified by environmental factors. For example, the child-rearing practices of parents can have a great effect in calming down a baby who is fractious and fearful, and in encouraging an infant who is inactive and moody.

Reinforcement of behaviour plays an important part in shaping a person's self-concept: if I am rewarded, as a child, for being kind and generous to other children, and I am rewarded regularly, then I will probably make a decision that this is behaviour to be repeated. (The reward may be a cuddle, or a kiss, or words of praise.) My self-concept then will include 'kind' and 'generous' as part of how I see myself — others have held a mirror to my actions to allow me to 'see' my behaviour the way that they see it.

During my early days — when I am a child — what those around me consider to be desirable behaviour is what will be reinforced in me, and is what will help to form my self-concept. The more experiences I have, the more chances I have to test my self and to receive feedback — from others out there — about my successes. My self-concept expands to include new information about who I am and what I can do.

But if my experiences are restricted, if, for example, my parents limit my opportunities to explore my environment because they fear for my safety, then any opportunities to enrich my self-concept are also limited. In this case, I may view myself as not able and even helpless.

If I am abandoned, if my basic needs are not met while I am still dependent on others to meet them, again my self-concept will suffer. In this case I may see myself as unworthy and unlovable.

Being authentic

To be authentic is to behave in harmony with one's inner sense of self. We may play roles at times, but as long as we are aware that the role is not who we actually are, and the role-playing is temporary, our authenticity remains intact. When we become the role, when we are immersed in playing a part and lose sense of who we really are, then we can feel a deep sense of alienation. This is the alienation of self from self: the distancing from the heart of who we are.

Sometimes, though, role-playing can be very constructive. It can allow us to try out different modes of behaviour and different ways of being with other people and with ourselves. It can, therefore, give us the opportunity to take risks we might not otherwise take.

For example, a shy person might be advised to act 'as if' they were outgoing and friendly for a week: the result, if they are courageous enough to take the risk, is that they experience what they may never have experienced before. By acting 'as if' they are outgoing, they receive feedback from the environment they have probably never received before. If the feedback is encouraging enough they may decide to break free from a limiting self-concept — 'I am shy' — and to practise reaching out to others more often.

A very outgoing person may try a similar exercise. Matt, a sociable, friendly young man, decided to try it for a week.

I did it for a particular reason, I must be honest. There were a couple of fellows at work who are quieter and keep to themselves more than I do, and I felt that they were being regarded as more serious workers, even though they weren't actually producing any more than I was.

It wasn't drastic, but I changed my behaviour slightly. I just quietened down, I talked less at morning tea time and just took more note of things like how other people were relating to each other, what people were wearing, the way they did little things. The funny thing was that a couple of people who had tended not to talk to me much actually approached me — my feeling is that they were intimidated by me when I talked and laughed a lot.

What Matt found through this exercise was that there was a side of him that had never been given the opportunity to develop: he saw that he could be quiet and observant just as he could be outgoing and entertaining. In trying something different he made some personal discoveries.

Rather than promoting inauthentic behaviour, what this approach can do is to help us understand who we are by exposing us to a greater variety of experiences and therefore a greater number of social mirrors which reflect back to us who we are in the context of other people.

LONELINESS AND SELF-ESTEEM
What is self-esteem?

While our self-concept refers to the way we *see* ourselves, self-esteem refers to the way we *feel* about ourselves.

Extensive research on the subject reveals a variety of results: for example, people with high self-esteem expect more acceptance and less rejection from others. Because they regard themselves in a positive way, they tend to see other people in a positive way, too.

In the same vein, individuals with low self-esteem are more sensitive to possible negative feedback than are those who have higher self-esteem. They will often look for cues that suggest they've failed, or haven't filled expectations. Feeling a sense of inferiority, they tend to feel threatened when they interact with someone they regard as superior in some way, possibly becoming quite defensive in response to the fear of possible judgement. Not convinced of their own standing, their beliefs and their values, they are more likely to be easily influenced by persuasive communications.

The results go on. What they all suggest is this — that it is through our self-esteem that we screen what we feel are other people's perceptions of us. If I feel poorly about myself, then I probably have difficulty accepting myself, and so my attitude may be: how could anyone else accept me?

If my self-esteem is low, then I would tend to be afraid to say how I really feel or think in case it displeases others and so I focus my behaviour on what others want. But even then I am not satisfied: even if another person seemed to like me, I would not believe it was possible.

This is classic self-defeating behaviour. The fact is that we can only believe positive feedback when we are sure that other people are seeing us as we really are. If we feel they are not seeing who we really are, then the feedback counts for nothing apart from possibly a momentary stroke of the ego. How can I take genuine pleasure in a comment that is aimed at a mask I wear other than to be reassured that the mask is firmly in place?

In interactions with other people, if we are involved in self-focused thought — if we are more concerned with how what we are saying is being evaluated than we are with anything else at all — then we exacerbate our self-consciousness, already heightened because of our low self-esteem.

What happens during times of self-focus is that the other person's behaviour is essentially ignored. The consequence here is obvious: the other person is getting no feedback of any sort from us. Is this real communication? Hardly. What it is, rather, is a superficial exchange that lacks meaning and genuine contact.

When self-esteem is low, we tend to look to others to provide good feelings rather than rely on ourselves. Dependency on others increases, as does sensitivity to any signs of disapproval.

Little wonder, then, that those with low self-esteem tend towards feelings of great loneliness. Cut off from their essential selves, trying hard to live up to an image of being socially correct and acceptable, intensely sensitive to others' reactions, generally disbelieving of any good feedback, they experience an emotional isolation that can become intolerable.

A common result

The correlation between extreme loneliness and low self-esteem is a regular finding of loneliness studies. Loneliness has been linked to self-criticism, to self-depreciation, to a lack of certainty of self-perception, to feeling unattractive and stupid.

Those with low self-esteem tend to be more passive and less popular in social settings, more socially anxious and not as likely to take risks. The result is that they are not likely to begin new relationships or to try enriching already existing relationships.

Low self-esteem may actually contribute to the persistence of loneliness over long periods, too. One study,[3] for example, found that self-esteem, amongst other factors, strongly influenced whether new college students experienced only transitory or more prolonged loneliness over the seven months of the research study.

Interestingly, the results of this study indicated that the lonely students tended to believe that they needed to be romantically attached to overcome loneliness and they also believed that the loneliness was their own fault rather than due to any environmental situation such as large, impersonal classes, or living in a dormitory.

The issue of romantic attachment is an interesting one: is it related to a need to experience the safety and security craved for in the early years of life? Is it a reliving of separation anxiety, experienced originally in infancy, and quelled only by the close contact of a special other? Is it a consequence of the influence of strong societal messages: that romance equals intimacy and genuine contact? Is it the symptom of a search for external reasons for the loneliness?

No doubt all of these factors are at play to some extent.

Low self-esteem — cause or consequence?

While it seems obvious that those individuals suffering low self-esteem would also suffer loneliness, we have to consider the possibility that low self-esteem is not only a cause but also a consequence of loneliness.

Early this century, William James[4] wrote that self-esteem is 'a fraction of which our pretensions are the denominator, and the numerator our success; thus self-esteem = success/pretensions'. What he meant was that the greater the discrepancy between our personal ideals (our pretensions) and our accomplishments (our success) the lower our self-esteem.

There is a mediating factor, however. If the lack of success is regarded as the result of outside causes, then self-esteem tends to be unaffected. Joan, a university lecturer, gives an example here.

I am always interested to note the types of students who blame their lack of success academically on causes other than lack of ability or lack of application.

Sometimes I am actually relieved that they use the excuses that they do — you know the sort of thing, tensions in the family, worry about finances, breaking up with a partner — because at least then they don't fall completely in a heap. There are outside causes to blame instead.

I am not saying that these things don't cause great stress and affect a student's final result, but in some cases it really is because of reasons they won't face up to. It can be hard for some people to accept that they aren't as bright as they think they are.

As Joan indicates in her comments, if failure is put down to personality characteristics or to lack of ability, self-esteem can be very much damaged. Unfortunately this is exactly what happens with chronically lonely people.

Whatever the situation that causes the initial feelings of loneliness, chronically lonely people start to believe that it is no longer a plausible reason and they begin to consider possibilities like lack of social skills and being unattractive. This puts in motion a vicious cycle: they begin to feel even less like initiating contact with others, they feel extremely anxious about communicating, and they start to question the point of interacting anyway. The result is a plummet in already shaky self-esteem.

Changing our self-view

There are various circumstances under which we lose people close to us. Divorce or death or separation mean that not only might we lose someone to whom we were attached (even in an unsatisfactory relationship), but we lose the social scaffolding that goes with that relationship.

May's story illustrates the loss involved when she talks about the personal devastation she felt when her husband left the family 'to sort things out', only to begin a new relationship with a female co-worker soon afterwards.

It wasn't only that he walked away without a second

glance, without any regrets for the loss of what we'd had all those years. It was so many other things. It was this feeling that I didn't know who I was anymore — me, May, who has always been so confident and competent! He has said that was part of the problem, of course. Well, he would have been happy afterwards, because I fell in a heap emotionally, I didn't feel confident and competent in any way!

I thought we'd built a life together and we'd made plans for the future, for when the kids had their own lives to lead. So the future was lost, too. I did a lot of grieving and I was very lonely, unbearably lonely, but finally I got to work building myself up from scratch, or so it seemed to me at the time.

Loss of this type often requires a reconstruction. As May's story reveals, not only does one's place in the social structure change dramatically, but personal identity is also threatened and can even be destroyed in the eyes of the grieving person. Whereas beforehand an identity was defined to some extent by that other who is now gone, it often needs rebuilding.

While this can be an extremely constructive exercise requiring, as it does, some thorough soul-searching as to who we are, where we've been and where we are heading, it may mean at least an initial drop in self-esteem as we come to terms with ourselves and our new situation.

FEELINGS OF SHAME AND ANXIETY
Loneliness, inferiority and shame

The images that the word 'loneliness' most commonly evokes are sad and sometimes even distasteful. Some of us may recoil from very lonely individuals, at best feeling compassion from a distance, at worst disdain for fellow humans who have allowed themselves to be so degraded.

It is largely because of the perceived need to be sociable, to have a large circle of friends and to be besieged with invitations to prove one's popularity, that to mention any feeling of loneliness is taboo. To be lonely is to have no friends, to have no social life, to have no identity, to be uninteresting, to be a social outcast of sorts. In other words, to be without friends, a partner or family is to be a failure and to admit to feeling lonely is to admit to being inadequate. One particular study revealed that individuals who live by themselves are regarded as 'lonely losers', and as personalities, they are cold, unfriendly and unattractive.[5]

Ours is essentially a gregarious society, emphasising interaction with others and the importance of friends and acquaintances. Media representations of happy, satisfied people invariably present them surrounded by others and enjoying their company.

Young people are particularly vulnerable to this concept of how life should be. Eager to be accepted, desperate to be one of the group, some will go to great lengths with their social life. Their lives may seem chaotic as they throw themselves into a frenzy of activities to be part of the group. Others sink into depression and label themselves as social and personal failures.

Research does indicate that young people experience more loneliness and other negative moods if they are on their own on Friday and Saturday nights. The researchers themselves comment:

> This magnified loneliness indicates the strong role played
> by sociocultural norms. Aloneness, at least in these
> circumstances, is heavily influenced by cultural
> prescriptions.[6]

It is these prescriptions that underpin the shame and anxiety these young people, and others, feel about their situation.

Loneliness has long been associated with a lack of being loved or wanted. The consequence, for those who experience the stirrings of loneliness, is strong feelings of inferiority. As

Thomas Wolfe describes it: 'Forever and forever in our loneliness, shameful feelings of inferiority will rise up suddenly to overwhelm us in a poisonous flood of horror, disbelief, and desolation ...'[7]

Shame plays a large part in the fear of revealing loneliness. We have been trained early in the importance of an acceptable persona, and in the importance of what our relatives and friends and neighbours think of us. Consequently we are quick to judge ourselves before others do it first. So much energy goes into maintaining an image of non-loneliness that there is little if any left to deal with the feeling itself.

Work up enough courage to tell someone, and chances are the same glib suggestions trip off the tongue: join a club and meet new people; change your job; stop being so housebound; be more outgoing; show your interest in other people by smiling and encouraging them to talk to you ...

While these words of advice can certainly be of some help in some situations, they can actually intensify the feelings of loneliness, partly because they don't address the underlying reason, and partly because we've not been rewarded for the risk we've taken in disclosing our problem.

It is clear that the person we've confided in about this loathed condition is not really listening or understanding. Further shame follows, deeper feelings of humiliation and despair, an even greater sense of alienation and estrangement.

Using shame as a guide
Shame as a negatively guiding principle has been the subject of discussion for some time.

All children depend on their parents for survival and to have their basic needs met. When these needs are only partially met, children are said to be neglected; when the needs are not met at all, they are abandoned. In a family where children are either neglected or abandoned, the children may grow up adapting to the situation through role-playing to help keep the family together and balanced.

Absorbing the uneasy atmosphere and picking up on the unexpressed emotions of their parents and other family members, they look for cues to tell them what role is most effective for them. Examples of roles might be the high achiever, or the caregiver, or the scapegoat. By taking on these roles to please parents, or to satisfy their parents' needs, children lose touch with who they really are — their authentic self.

Alienated from their authentic self, and interpreting their abandonment as being due to lack of worth, they feel a great sense of shame about themselves. This shame takes over the whole identity so that a human being feels flawed and defective. And very lonely.

This is shame in the context of neglected or abandoned childhood leading to unhealthy relating later on. But, taken out of this arena, shame can be a healthy human emotion. Rather than viewing it as a stumbling block to freedom and self-expression, we can regard it as essential to our development and maturity as human beings. As one writer on the subject says: '[Shame] reveals the limits of the self and bears witness to the self's involvement with others. Shame thus functions as a guide to a more authentic form of self-realisation.'[8]

It would seem that for those who feel lonely, there are two layers of difficulty. The first is the loneliness itself, the feeling of isolation or inner emptiness or whatever else it may mean for the individual at that particular time.

The second layer is the shame associated with the loneliness, the shame of being inadequate or faulty in some way, of being somehow dissociated from the rest of humanity with no obvious hope of being reconnected quickly and painlessly. In other words, not only is there the loneliness to handle, but there is the shame as well.

It is the shame that drives us to develop and present popular, busy and sociable personas, the type that could never be lonely. It is the shame that keeps us from admitting openly how alienated we feel. It is the shame that disempowers us so that our frightened little selves cringe at the thought that we may be unmasked and revealed for what we are: lonely and alone.

Ironically, the shame of feeling lonely can have the effect of making us more lonely, and so more ashamed, and so more lonely, and so more ashamed, and so the cycle spins on and on until it is quite out of control, and we are quite out of control with it. The consequence is anxiety, sometimes in quite extreme form, which can go so far as to immobilise us.

It is interesting to note how often we are weighed down or immobilised by a secondary response such as anxiety: feeling lonely, for example, can become an extremely complex experience when shame and anxiety, and possibly other feelings as well, are part of the package. The trick is to get to the core of the problem and deal with that, or else inestimable energy goes into dealing with the secondary emotions.

But view shame simply as a sign of our humanity, and as an indication of the extent of our relationship with others and with what some refer to as the Other, and it takes on a fresh connotation. It is a measure of our self-consciousness, and a measure of our awareness of prevailing social values.

The shame that we feel on recognising our loneliness is an opportunity in itself to question our own personal values and our interpretations of personal experience. What does it mean to be lonely? we can ask ourselves. How do I present myself to the rest of the world, and how does this loneliness fit in with that? Is my loneliness something to be kept unexpressed and concealed, something to be dealt with in private only?

More than one writer has questioned the push towards eradicating shame altogether from our lives because of what are regarded widely as its crippling and inhibitive effects. We may choose to see it as an important dimension of our experience in that it emphasises our vulnerability and allows us an understanding of true and full humanity. 'Because of its particular dynamics, shame has a singular capacity to disclose the self to the self ... Through the experience of shame, identity may not only be confirmed, but shaped, enlarged, and put into perspective.'[9]

This attitude encourages a gentler approach to ourselves when feelings of shame complicate the feelings of loneliness, and it presents the opportunity for much greater self-awareness through the exploration of both layers.

UNMET EXPECTATIONS
Social expectations

If we want to understand our loneliness and meet it head on, we need to consider the possibility that we hold expectations that are not being realised and possibly never can be.

We all have expectations, whether or not we are aware of them. For example, we assume that most people around us are socialised beings and that they will behave in a socialised way in public: the person sitting next to me on the train in the morning won't spit at my feet, nor will my neighbour toss rubbish over our boundary fence and into my property.

Many of our expectations of this sort make for good social order — social manners, including respect for others and their property, help life run smoothly for us all, and it is fair that we have expectations that those around us will co-operate so that we can all live peacefully, at least on that level.

Some expectations are born of a different culture, a different time, a different place. The generation gap has caused ripples since time immemorial, with elders complaining bitterly about the behaviour of the young, and young people becoming even more rebellious at the idea that they are not living up to expectations.

Older people particularly can fall into deep despair about what it will all mean for the future: here is a generation of the young openly defying what for them have been some of the basic tenets of a viable society. Here they are changing all the rules and, what's more, getting away with it.

Change, and especially social change, is a difficult process to accept and to cope with. Why should anyone else change rules that seem to have worked well for many a decade? Why should the code of dress that seemed perfectly respectable and attractive be changed for no obvious reason? Why aren't the elders being treated with respect and asked to speak forth the wisdom they so dearly want to pass on?

The answers to these questions, such as they are, contain an element of sadness, mainly because the 'elders' of our society are not seen in the same light as the elders of tribes or even the elders in some eastern cultures. Our society has less structure than those others and the wisdom of years of experience that our elders have is less highly regarded.

But the answers also contain an element of optimism: if our elders treasure the wisdom they do hold, and if at the same time they accept the change around them with some graciousness, they will help lead the young into a more confident and stable future for themselves. Where resentment and judgement widen rifts and undermine relationships between old and young, kindness and acceptance together with strength of will can lovingly bridge the gap.

Feeling disappointed

One therapist claims that those clients who come to him complaining of loneliness over an extended period of time tend to set expectations of their friends and their partners that are quite unrealistic.[10] These are the clients who are easily insulted, who feel frustrated by and disappointed in their friends, although they insist that all they want is that people do what is only reasonable.

Those who meet these same clients outside the therapy room would describe them as rigid and stubborn, demanding and moralistic. The lonely clients certainly don't see themselves in this way at all — in fact, they often feel that they are excellent friends, loyal and supportive, dependable and approachable.

It is worrying to think that we don't see ourselves as others see us.

Could we be one of those the therapist describes? Quite possibly, although people who are as inflexible as they seem would not spend too much time on self-reflection and understanding. Usually their main priority is to find out what is wrong with other people: how can they be so selfish? insensitive? uncaring? Don't they see how lonely I am? If they would just change their behaviour ...

It is up to each of us to examine our expectations when we feel disappointed in others. Are they reasonable expectations? They may be, especially when basic personal principles are concerned, or where basic human respect is involved. The test may be, in the end, whether we seem to have lost friends, or not attracted them, over some time. If this is the case, it may be that we have expectations that other people find impossible to satisfy.

There are some exceptions. Take Rebecca's story:

> For years I felt like everybody's doormat. It took me a long time to realise it, but I was following in my mother's shadow, doing what she had done, allowing other people to demand of me until there was nothing left to give. With a lot of determination and some help from a counsellor, I crawled out of the hole I felt I was in. It was slow and sometimes painful — my friends noticed I wasn't the Rebecca they had always known, and it was awful pushing people out of my life even temporarily so that I could find out who I was.
>
> Now that I've come out at the other end, I can say that it was mostly worth it. I say mostly because I still have to work hard at what I call 'the new me' which isn't really that at all — it's just the real me who was buried.

For Rebecca, 'losing' friends and acquaintances was part of a big upheaval for her, a personal renewal that was essential. They were not lost because of her expectations of them, but because she needed to find herself — she felt that she had been buried under all the expectations others had of her.

Expectations, social or personal, can weigh heavily. They can trap us into a cycle of self-destructive behaviour from which there is no escape unless, like Rebecca, we fight our way out of the hole.

And they can disappoint us deeply when others don't fall in with what we believe to be 'right behaviour'. Whether we respond by turning inwards, vowing never to trust again, or whether we decide to confront and ask why our expectations aren't being met, or whether we decide to reflect on whether or not those expectations are reasonable, is a personal choice. Like all choices, it has its consequences.

However, blaming others for our sense of isolation and deep feelings of loneliness is a dead-end street. Examining our expectations more closely and choosing to let go as long as our sense of identity is intact and not too threatened by such an approach, is more likely to open up both ends to traffic.

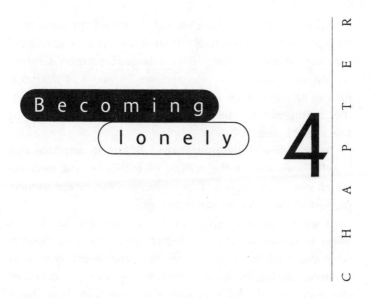

DEVELOPMENTAL ASPECTS
Becoming attached

It is widely considered that loneliness in adulthood has its roots in early childhood experiences and the theory of attachment — as proposed by John Bowlby — helps to explain how this might happen.

Bowlby believed that 'affectional bonding' — the bonding to significant others in our lives — is part of our biological makeup, existing as it does in a variety of species of bird and mammal. For this reason, social attachments — the ties that bind us to our most intimate companions — have been explained in terms of evolutionary theory. That is, all animals, including human beings, have innate behavioural tendencies as part of their evolutionary heritage, and the purpose of these tendencies is to increase the chances of survival for all.

The way this would happen would be that the attached caregiver would serve to protect the young from discomfort and from predators. Considering the longer term, the young would be surer to live long enough to ensure the survival of the species by reproducing. What is essential to affectional bonding, Bowlby wrote, 'is that bonded partners tend to remain in proximity to one another ... many of the most intense of our human emotions arise during the formation, the maintenance, the disruption, and the renewal of affectional bonds.'[1]

Associated with the most intense of human emotions that Bowlby mentions is the feeling of loneliness and isolation which has been explained as replicating earlier experience: the loss of close ties, or the fear of it.

It was during his early research on loneliness that Robert Weiss happened to attend a lecture given by John Bowlby who discussed his writings on the attachment system in children. During the lecture, Bowlby began to give details of the response of children who feel that they have been abandoned by their parents. Weiss later recalled that the description included these sorts of reactions: the child's total energies being taken up in trying to regain their parents, their tension and their fear, their restlessness and watchfulness as they awaited their parents' return. As he sat in the audience, Weiss wrote later, he felt like a cartoon character with a newly lit bulb above his head.

'I realized that the loneliness whose nature had been puzzling me was exactly the state that Bowlby was describing, except that it occurred with adults and that it had no particular lost figure on whom to focus.'[2] Weiss later described loneliness as 'separation distress without an object'. It seemed a perfectly accurate description to him.

He went on to say that it is his belief that, during adolescence, the attachment system is modified so that the original object of the attachment — the parents or parent — is replaced. For example, all the behaviour associated with 'falling in love' — the suspension of reality, the attention focused on the loved one — may be explained as an integration of new attachment figures.

Certainly Bowlby believed that through early experiences we develop an attachment style that we maintain throughout our lives. His view has been supported by a number of longitudinal and retrospective studies,[3] and the effect of this attachment style on the experience of adult romantic love has also been explored.[4] One of the factors affecting the development of attachment style is our experience of separation during our early years.

Separation anxiety

The first few months are an extremely important time in the life of the infant. These months provide time for those aspects that establish the solidity of the relationship — warmth, consistency and closeness.

During this time, infants pass through particular stages as part of the development of close ties with their caregivers. Notice the term 'caregivers' rather than just 'mothers': it has been argued often that the important role of fathers in the nurturing care of their children has been overlooked. Certainly in the past the importance of fathers as attachment objects and as contributors to the social and emotional development of their children was considered marginal. These days we know better, and in fact research tells us that a child's secure attachment to father, as well as mother, means that the child will be more socially responsive and less fearful in strange surroundings.

All the same, it seems that even when father stays at home to be the child's primary caregiver, mother is still the one seen to be the more nurturing and comforting caregiver in most cases.

Because it is most usually the mother who provides close contact and nurturance from the time of birth, we will continue to refer specifically to her role in the context of primary caregiving — we will assume that she is the one who most often feeds the infant, holds it close and fondles it most, seeks eye contact and reacts warmly to her child's responses.

For their first few months of life, infants are beginning to discriminate between certain people, so that between three and six months of age, they are more likely to respond to their mothers with a smile than to people who are not familiar to them. They are also more quickly soothed by a regular caregiver than by anyone else. It is around the age of seven months that infants begin to show discomfort and distress when they are separated from their mothers or fathers, or from other people who are familiar to them.

Anyone who has baby-sat a small child knows the distressed reaction that follows mother and father leaving for a night out: as they prepare to leave, the child becomes anxious and clingy, anticipating the imminent separation.

Separation anxiety peaks between fourteen and twenty months, and eases over the ensuing months, so that by pre-school age the reaction is less intense and also less frequent.

Separation is not always cause for anxiety and distress. Take the case of Stephanie, who is almost a year old: she is playing with her toys in the same room as her mother who is talking with a friend of hers. Her mother stands at one point and, taking up her bag, leaves the room. Stephanie becomes agitated and begins to crawl towards the door after her mother, whimpering until she arrives there, and, her mother not in sight, she starts to cry and is inconsolable until her mother returns.

Let's run through another scene: Stephanie is playing in the same room as her mother and then starts to crawl towards the door as her mother continues her conversation with a friend. Every so often, Stephanie stops to look around at her mother, then continues out of the room into the hall to play with some toys that are scattered there. She can't see her mother from where she is sitting, but she is perfectly happy.

Although small children react with distress when their mother or close caregiver leaves them, they are much more relaxed about separations that they themselves intitiate. However, they will move back towards a caregiver if a stranger appears, or if the caregiver moves away while the child is in the process of exploring their environment.

If a stranger appeared in the hall where Stephanie was playing, for example, the little girl would immediately turn and retreat to her mother's side. And if she heard her mother move away from where she had been sitting, perhaps walking in a direction away from Stephanie, that too would send her rushing back to find her mother.

The extent of the reaction to separation can be quite severe, with the infant expressing emotions as extreme as rage and despair — here are the intense human emotions that Bowlby mentioned.

It is up to the caregivers themselves to be aware of the anxiety of separation and to alleviate it where they can. In Stephanie's case, for example, by staying put while her baby girl explored her surroundings her mother would be providing a secure base for her child to explore the unknown and start to feel more at ease in the environment. With this familiarity, Stephanie would become more and more able to cope with separation and more confident in the face of strangers and strange places.

It would be rare for any infant or toddler never to be left by their mother or other caregiver. There has been a dramatic rise in employment over the last twenty years or so amongst women who are mothers, which means that more and more young children have experienced day care. Even among young children whose mothers are not working outside the home most are left at some stage with a babysitter for at least a short time. Even when the sitter is a relative or close friend of the parents, the child may not feel the same strong bond with them.

While the separations we have considered so far have been short-term, sometimes young children are separated from their loved ones for a prolonged period. John Bowlby looked into this more than thirty years ago when he considered the behaviour of children who were aged between fifteen and thirty months and who were suffering chronic illness in hospital.

He talked of three phases that the children passed through during their separation: the first was the protest phase, during which time the child cried and resisted the efforts of other caregivers. The second was the phase of despair, when the child seemed to have no hope of being together with mother again. They seemed to be 'in a deep state of mourning'. The third phase Bowlby called the stage of detachment, when the child began to show renewed interest in other people and in playing, but was indifferent when the mother appeared, and barely protested when she left again.

Research since Bowlby's indicates that children who have a secure attachment to their mother or father or other caregivers may well protest and despair over separation that is long-term, but are unlikely to detach themselves from these close others. Those with insecure attachments, though, are more likely to distance themselves, or even withdraw altogether from human contact.

Attachment styles

In line with this research, three main styles of attachment have been identified by one group of researchers in their observations of parent–infant interactions.[5]

The first of these styles is 'secure attachment' and is the result of available and responsive caregiving. The second is 'anxious/ambivalent attachment' and is the result of anxious caregiving: in this case, the caregiver is at some times available to the child and at other times unavailable (perhaps emotionally rather than physically) or intrusive. Children raised under these circumstances are being what is called 'partially reinforced' so that their style is to be anxious and clingy and to feel fearful about the possibility of separation or withdrawal of affection. The third style is 'avoidant attachment' and is the result of an unresponsive or even rejecting caregiver.

These patterns, practised over a long enough period of time, become part of the personality pattern and so are carried into the concept of self that we develop and into our style of relating to others. Various studies reveal the relationship between attachment style and loneliness after childhood.

A parent–child relationship that is less than satisfactory increases the probability of loneliness in adulthood, as a study of over 500 college students has revealed.[6] The same study showed that those with unsatisfactory parent relationships were more introverted and suffered lower self-esteem than those who enjoyed satisfactory relationships with their parents. Another study, conducted in 1986,[7] revealed that childrearing practices, and most particularly a lack of positive involvement of parents with their children, were related to the loneliness of offspring later on.

An interesting aspect of the 'anxious/ambivalent' style is that parental intrusion can have the same effect as being unavailable to the child. In a study of 207 elderly women in Stockholm in 1987,[8] it was found that where there had been some degree of parental intrusion — in particular, a mother who was over-involved to the point of limiting the child's ability to develop in an independent and autonomous way — the outcome was 'narcissism' and an associated loneliness.

Could it be that too much involvement can be just as damaging and far-reaching in its consequences as can too little care and attention? Could it be that, whether the infant/child is neglected or overprotected, the essential outcome is the same: the self of the young person is not given the opportunity to 'complete' with the bonding process?

In the case of the neglected, there may ensue a life-long need for attachment in order to bring back what was once lost. The need may not always be obvious, or even in action, and may emerge at times of insecurity or threat. The overprotected, on the other hand, may never experience their own power and strength of will, and may feel that hope and safety lie only in the attachment to others. Their underlying conflict may lie in wanting to be free and independent while at the same time fearing the possibility of being alone in the world.

Unmet needs in infancy and childhood — we are talking here about the basic needs for contact, intimacy and social stimulation — can lead to psychological hunger just as lack of food leads to physiological hunger. The suggestion is that for those individuals whose needs were not met early in their lives the hunger emerges in adulthood as the experience of loneliness.

The picture may look grim for those of us who feel that our attachment style has been other than secure, but even if we have not discovered it for ourselves or seen it happen in those around us, there is evidence to indicate that the style can be changed. If the circumstances of parents change, and they moderate their own style in relation to their children, the attachment behaviour of the child will change.[9] For example, if certain stresses are lifted from parents — they become financially secure where beforehand they have been stressed by insufficient finances in raising their children, for instance — and if those parents also put more energy and time into their children, those children will gradually become more secure in their feelings of attachment.

Despite the tendency for our own attachment styles to be perpetuated in our children, there is evidence that there are those adults who have experienced quite disturbed relationships with their own parents and, establishing a secure style for themselves in later years, now enjoy a secure relationship with their children.[10] This can most usually be achieved by recognising and accepting early negative experiences and deciding to consciously work on a way of relating to our children that is different from our own experience with our parents. Guided help — in the form of therapy — is often essential when early experiences have been disturbing and distressing.

EARLY DAYS
Loneliness in the young

Although it has been suggested that the potential for loneliness starts to develop just before adolescence when youngsters begin to feel the need for intimate others in their lives,[11] it is more likely that very small children can feel lonely, especially if they are socially isolated. Certainly many people remember feeling lonely either once in a while or quite regularly when they were very young. 'I didn't know what to call it then,' one fifteen-year-old boy says, 'but now I would call it loneliness.'

Assuming that young children can feel lonely, their loneliness may be different in some respects from the loneliness of older people, whether adolescents or adults. All the same, whatever the reason, children who have no friends may feel bored and alienated, excluded and rejected — painful feelings that relate to a deep sense of loneliness.

This is not to say that young children who do seem to have friendships never experience some feelings of loneliness: however, because they are not yet practised in putting a particular word to a feeling, it's hard to say whether this is the case.

The effects of social isolation can be profound for young children, just as they can be for adults. Why do they experience social isolation? There may be several different reasons.

The first of these is that some children find it difficult to make friends or to maintain a friendship because they do not have the necessary social skills. It would be easy to dismiss the need for friendships at this age, but that would be to deny their importance in so many ways: our self-concept, for example, depends very much on how our peers regard us and treat us from an early age.

Anyone who has watched pre-schoolers at play would know how much work goes into relationship-building. Some children are simply better at it than others, and they seem to know instinctively what is needed to make a friend, or to soothe ruffled feathers.

Take this example straight from the pre-school playroom: Jessie, a four-year-old, has used bits and pieces from the dress-up box to adorn herself and begins to strut across the room looking very colourful.

'You look dumb,' Jack says to her.

'I don't look dumb. I'm a special person,' Jessie replies with a toss of her head.

'No, you just look dumb,' Jack insists.

'Stop, Jack. I don't! I'm a special person.' Jessie's lip begins to tremble.

'Well, you look dumb, and so do I,' Jack says, picking up a length of rag lying nearby and draping it over his head. Both children burst into laughter.

Jack had noticed the trembling lip and, not wanting his friend to be hurt, turned the situation around so that they could both see the funny side of it. He showed great skill and resourcefulness, and, after a shaky start, sensitivity to another's feelings.

There are many skills to master at a young age: we have to learn how to be included in group activities, and how to show approval and support to our peers. We also need to know how to cope with conflict and to manage it, and how to be sensitive and tactful when it is necessary.

It isn't all that easy learning these skills, and putting them into practice can be difficult too. If we observe young children's behaviour we would notice that if two or more children define an activity and structure it in a particular way, then they will often exclude others who try to join in later.

It would take extraordinary skills, then, to gain entry into this activity, so that even a child who was quite skilled at forming friendships generally speaking, would find it difficult to be included in this setup.

'Two is company, three is a crowd' applies even at this age — a third child trying to join in what an established couple is involved in may feel quite ostracised, even when just yesterday the three were the best of friends. As we grow older we learn to share more, and to include others even though we would rather not; the rule of 'Do unto others ...' is often a common theme during primary school years.

Several studies report what we all know from experience: that the children likely to be most popular with others tend to be those who are most attentive to other children, give them praise and fall in with their requests.

It could be argued that these are the children who are most socialised, having learnt what works well in the social environment and applying their learned skills to be rewarded with ample opportunities for friendship.

Are these children who will develop into those adults who, driven by a sense of loneliness, try too hard for friendship? Are these the 'other-directed' people we talked of in Chapter Two, the ones who pick up cues about how to behave to be liked and accepted?

This is likely if, at an early age, they put all their energies into others, so keen are they for acceptance and affection. If they start then to define themselves in terms of satisfying other people's needs, without a true sense of themselves as individuals with their own needs and desires, then this may well become their way of relating generally.

While socialisation is essential for anyone who is going to live effectively and satisfyingly amongst other people, it can be carried to extremes. Parents or even teachers or child-care workers may in some circumstances tend to overlook children's needs for autonomy and individuality, and for the expression of a wide range of emotions, including anger.

The expression of anger is very important to children's development. When they can't perform a task, for example, or when parents restrict their behaviour, or when they experience rivalry with a sibling or with a peer, they may feel angry, and while that is understandable, the hostility that emerges with the angry feelings may be difficult for adults to handle.

To be told angrily that they are not to express anger leaves them unsure and confused; to be punished tells them that they are not valued and that to express such feelings may mean a withdrawal of love. The fear of such consequences may be enough to teach them to suppress all 'negative' emotions and to appear cheerful and friendly under all circumstances. We all know about the shame that can grow out of feeling emotions that are considered 'off-limits', and the loneliness that results from keeping them hidden away in the dark.

To see anger expressed cleanly and openly, with no blame attached and with a healthy resolution, is a great help to children's development. If they are allowed to express their anger in a loving atmosphere, without destruction or complete loss of control, they learn to respect themselves and their own feelings, and they are more likely to feel clear about where they stand in terms of others. They are more likely to be attentive to other people, too, to praise them generously and to fall in with their requests because they have a healthy enough self-esteem to reach out to others, and not because they know no other way to be accepted and loved.

Predictably, children who will not co-operate with others, or who ignore or ridicule, are likely to be least popular. This is not to say that a child who seems 'unpopular' is necessarily displaying this kind of behaviour in the playground: there are often a number of prevailing factors. Toni tells of her experience as a young child:

When I was about five years old, we moved to a new suburb and I went off to the local infants' school. I was quite shy, but not so shy that I couldn't try to join in on games. There was this girl, I remember, who was a little older and a real bully, and she decided to take a dislike to me. She told some kids in my class that I smelt, that I was freaky ... different things that I couldn't defend myself against. More and more, the other kids were staying away from me.

Then, suddenly, she left the school. Oh, luck! Everything changed, and I played in several different groups. In fact, one of my closest girlfriends after all these years is from way back then in kindergarten.

Defending ourselves against others who, like the girl at Toni's school, use power over others to derive satisfaction, is difficult enough when we are mature and more sure of ourselves. For a tiny person it can be an impossible task.

Toni's long-term friendship from those very early years is an indication of how important those early relationships can be at the time. And for those adolescents and adults who enjoy friendship over such a long span of time, there is a particular sense of continuity in their lives and a shared history that can provide a great feeling of security.

Skills of interaction

Developing the skills of friendship starts early, and opportunities to interact with peers gives a headstart: it is with peers that children learn, largely through trial and error, what works and what doesn't. It is through playing with others that the subtle skills of conflict management are honed down and the use of tact to prevent hurt feelings practised.

It is through their peers that children learn many of their interaction skills, but there are times when they do need help from parents or teachers or other 'elders'. Intervention may be essential in cases where children are caught in a vicious circle: lacking friends, they lack the self-confidence that develops through friendship, and lacking self-confidence they hold back from approaching others with whom they would like to be friendly.

An adult might intervene by encouraging interaction with a particular other child, or by subtly teaching new social skills that may be lacking. It is important, though, for adults to be aware of their own motivation: we need to respect the differences between children and to accept that some prefer to spend a lot of time on their own rather than be 'outgoing and sociable' by others' standards and expectations.

Jeremy, who is eighteen and recently finished high school, comments on the struggle he had to convince his family that he really does enjoy his solitude. His parents entertain a great deal, both formally and informally, and they have always had very many social commitments. Their older daughter is very sociable, in their sense of the word, but Jeremy does not fit the mould.

> I think they have the message now. For years I've enjoyed bushwalking, maybe with just one other person, or working on my artwork in my room. They wanted to send me to a counsellor years ago, but the school counsellor told them there is nothing to worry about and that at school I got on with people and wasn't at all withdrawn, which is what they thought.

Because of their ideas of sociability, Jeremy's parents saw him as withdrawn because he had different needs from theirs. These days they accept him more, and appreciate that he enjoys his own company enormously, although occasionally they do ask themselves where they went wrong.

Playing is serious

While we watch Jessie and Jack 'playing' at pre-school, dressing up, scrambling over climbing frames, pretending, and joining in various other activities, they are actually learning at a great rate.

Babies begin to play very early in life, manipulating objects end enjoying peek-a-boo games with others, and when they are around twelve months of age they start on pretend play. Children of pre-school age who pretend a lot in their play tend to be more popular with their peers and more socially mature.[12] It would seem then that play activities lead to the development of social skills.

Play serves another purpose: it helps a child cope with

emotional crises and serves to reduce conflict. Piaget[13] has pointed out that during the socialisation process, children are required to adapt to a world that can be upsetting. During symbolic play emotional conflicts will often emerge, so that if, for example, a child is disciplined at lunchtime, within a couple of hours the interaction will be played out with dolls and a happy resolution reached. Not only does symbolic play figure in the resolving of conflicts, Piaget believed, but it can also compensate for needs that are unsatisfied.[14]

Role-taking is also part of play — young children become Superman, WonderWoman, doctors, nurses, space travellers, mothers, fathers. This aspect of pretend play enables them to try out the roles that they see other people playing and in stepping into their shoes they are imagining how those individuals feel in those roles. The more advanced and sophisticated the role-taking, the more a child will be aware of the needs of others and the reasons that they may behave as they do.

In this way, children become more familiar with their social world, but they also add further dimensions to their self-concept.

The role of siblings

Ask any person about their childhood and chances are that, within a sentence or two, brother or sister has emerged as friend or foe, as vital to the process of growing up as anyone could be. The fact is that most of us grow up with siblings and we are likely to spend more time with them during our early years than we spend with our mother and father. Although they are rarely acknowledged as such, sibling relationships must surely be amongst our most influential and our most enduring.

The family structure is a mini-society within which our earliest experiences occur; it provides the perfect opportunity for each of us to learn to relate effectively with one another and to learn to resolve conflict in mutually satisfying ways.

Children with high self-esteem most often have close relationships with their bothers and sisters. Self-esteem established early in life tends to accompany us into adulthood and influence our dealings with other people.

Unfortunately, it also follows that early sibling rivalry that is never resolved, early competitiveness that becomes fiercer with each birthday, early ridicule or disdain that is never properly addressed by parents and which may, in fact, be provoked by parents, all lead to the poor self-esteem which can cause problems for us in adulthood.

In the social networks of old age, the sibling relationship is unique because of the history of shared lifetime experiences. A number of studies[15] have shown that elderly people who had positive sibling relationships reported that interactions with their brothers or sisters decreased feelings of loneliness and provided emotional support and closeness. What happens between siblings early in life is of great significance to them as they grow older, and closeness seems to be most pronounced in those families where the children spent time together: playing, eating, going to school, and sharing bedrooms.

Relationship dynamics between siblings can vary widely during a lifetime: critical events mean significant changes, and these events may be sickness, or the divorce or death of the parents, or the marriage of a sibling. It is the quality of the relationship before the event that will help determine the outcome — close and loving siblings will often become even closer, while rivalrous siblings will often experience even more conflict.

Sibling dynamics have shifted dramatically as a result of social change. For example, where forty or fifty years ago the number of children in a family may have been four or five or more, these days it is common for a child to have just one brother or sister. There is also an increasing tendency for one-child families. In the larger families of the past, siblings tended to create a subculture of their own, offering support and nurture to each other when mother and father were unable to spread themselves across so many. A study of large families[16] conducted in the 1950s revealed that most children saw being part of a large family as useful and important. They reported positive consequences, such as learning to share with others, the need to develop self-control and to be considerate to other people.

This same study, carried out by J. H. S. Bossard, revealed something that surprised psychiatrists of the time: many of the subjects from large families set great store by the security that their siblings provided them. This result flew in the face of 'common knowledge' — that a child's security is based almost entirely on the relationship between parent and child. Many subjects felt that their brothers and sisters understood far better than did their parents the problems they were likely to face as young people.

One young man, the seventh of eight children, speaks enthusiastically about being part of a large family.

> My brothers and sisters and I played a lot of sport together — we were together every day, caring for each other, supporting each other, sometimes fighting. Our parents were always there, too, but we related differently to them — their role was more important when one of us was sick, or when there was a birthday. Even now, if I feel a bit down, I can always turn to one of my siblings to talk about things. The bond is very strong between us.

While in larger groups chances are high that there is at least one other sibling with whom one can be particularly close and who can give support, couples of children are not afforded the same choice. Only children are in a unique position here. Because they have no siblings, they may miss out on the admiration, support, criticism and companionship that these special peers can offer and which help us to establish our identity in the world and in relation to one another. At the same time, most children these days are exposed to pre-school and other forms of childcare where they have the opportunity to meet and mix with a number of children of similar age. This experience can serve to offset the lack of peers at home.

Moving away, growing apart

The emotional response to moving away from friends, or a close friend moving away from us, is a sort of grief, which is not surprising when we consider that loss is involved. Feeling lonely and depressed and unsettled and even angry is quite a natural reaction to such loss, and can happen at any time in our lives. Small children are just as susceptible to these feelings as are adults, and, also like adults, the ways in which they come to terms with such change vary widely.

Children in general seem quite resilient: they gradually learn to adjust to the new situation and to establish at least one friendship as soon as they can. Not all children cope so well, though, and sometimes it can be a long time before they adjust and reach out.

While moving away physically can be a painful experience, so can growing apart. This tends to happen as children grow older, and as their needs and abilities and interests change. Friends who once provided satisfying relationships for each other start to drift apart, no longer sharing what once held them together. This is part of the waxing and waning of friendships in children, and is quite normal, but while they are probably quite necessary parts of growing up, some children find breaking up of friendship very difficult.

Eleven-year-old Karen talks about her experience:

I've been in this group for a while, but now everyone seems a bit unhappy. I think it's because some of us are interested in different sorts of things and the rest of the group is scared that it will break us up, which it will. A couple of the girls are still collecting dolls and a couple of them are talking about cute boys at school, and I'm one of the ones in the middle — I don't want us to break up because we've been friends for a while, and I don't know anyone else that well, but I can see it's going to happen.

The relationship break-up will be hard for Karen and her friends, but perhaps being able to reason out what is happening takes the edge off the hurt. Very young children are not able to talk about what is happening in the same way, or even to recognise what is going on, and consequently they can feel very hurt when a friend moves on to someone else. This is not an uncommon occurrence for four- and five-year-olds: a friend can want to move on to someone new and the child left behind can be devastated by what is perceived as rejection.

Pre-adolescence

Once overlooked as a period of any significance, the ages between about eight and twelve are when children are learning the fundamental skills of their culture. Whether it is schoolwork or other interests, these are the skills valued by society, and as children become more confident in them they start to see themselves more and more in the context of the larger community.

This is the time when children commit themselves to a social unit outside of, and larger than, the family unit. To begin with, as they interact with peers, they start to recognise the limits of their own point of view: other children may see things quite differently, and rather than being forced, perhaps, to accept adults' ideas, they are freer to argue with peers and to reach some final agreement, or compromise, for the sake of the friendship. In this sense they are moving away from the egocentrism of early childhood to a wider view of the world.

Leading up to adolescence, the peer group starts to become increasingly important, and where once energy would go into gaining the approval of the teacher, soon it is classmates whose approval is sought. They may take on roles to entertain their audience — the rest of the class. They may become the class clown, for example, or the social butterfly, or the class hero.

As approval becomes a more and more powerful need, children look to the norms of the group to conform to, and they may start to dress and talk in a particular way, and even to profess antagonism towards the opposite sex.

This is 'best friend' time, too, with same-sex friendships possibly becoming very intimate. All sorts of things happen within these relationships: secret codes, dangerous adventures, pledges of lifetime loyalty; fights, making up, reuniting ... The significance lies in children experiencing such closeness and affection for those their own age rather than adults, because the relationship can be experienced on the young person's own terms rather than in an adult context.

As with any stage of life, there are wide individual differences at this time. While some children will follow this stage through in a predictable pattern, there are those who develop the skills involved either earlier or later.

What matters is that we adults can accept the differences and the range of responses rather than allowing expectations to interfere with the natural evolving of a child's nature. Especially at a time when children are learning how to be in the world that is bigger than the home, we need to be sensitive to their rate of development and to their possible fears about that world.

When as adults we feel quite comfortable with solitude, or the feelings of loneliness that any human being might experience at times, we can convey that to the child, especially the one who finds it most difficult to conform to the group. For this child, it might be less a case of a lack of social skills and more a case of earlier-than-expected introspection, one of the hallmarks of adolescence.

Adolescence

LONELINESS IN ADOLESCENCE
The need to belong

During early adolescence — from about eleven years of age — peer approval begins to become more important than ever. At the same time, the young adolescent may feel pressured from various sources to be part of a group. Peers, parents, teachers, may all exert some pressure, however subtle, to join a group, thus aligning themselves with the entire social system which smiles on the individual who belongs to a group rather than the one who remains solitary and not affiliated.

This push may reflect what was discussed earlier: the high value that is placed on togetherness in most human societies, either for pure survival, or to provide the companionship it is commonly believed that human beings need. Whatever the case, the adolescent asks questions such as 'Who am I? Where do I belong?'

Casting an eye around the available social groupings, they think about their own needs and how they would fit into this group or that. It is a happy event if they find, or happen to fall in with, a group that provides a sense of belonging for them, because it is this that helps them grow psychologically and provides a basis for success at this stage of their lives.

If, on the other hand, an adolescent does not ever experience a sense of belonging in any group, then they are bound to feel alienated, and a vicious cycle may be set in motion: not finding a place in any particular social grouping, they may conclude that they have nothing to offer and may refrain from further attempts to belong.

The need to belong may be so strong that young people try to achieve it at any cost. They may grab the first chance to belong somewhere, however harmful it may be in the longer term.

The value of the peer group lies in its power to expand feelings of self-worth and to allay any feelings of loneliness. However, for someone to belong to such a group, there has to be some suppression of individuality — not necessarily a great deal, because the life of the group often depends very much on the differences amongst its members, allowing specific roles to emerge which help define the group.

But every group has its norms, and to conform to these is to show commitment to the group. In fact, some conformity is a healthy sign: it provides security and it gives the adolescent the chance to demonstrate that s/he belongs somewhere.

Peer pressure is most often discussed in a negative context, implying the destructive effects it can have on a young person and the measure of insecurity it reveals when an individual succumbs to it. However, peer pressure has a positive role to play in the development of an adolescent: being part of any group entails expectations, or peer pressure from other members, to exhibit qualities that may not be obviously there. Needing to act as if more confident and more outgoing, more courageous and more assertive, provides the opportunity to experience new personal dimensions. Satisfying these expectations can have a wonderful effect on the adolescent's self-image because it can actually expand the sense of self.

Sometimes, though, the expectations of the group can cause unbearable tension because the adolescent feels that those expectations are far too removed from their own values. Pulling away from the group may keep personal values intact, but it means alienation to some extent because, as we become more autonomous, thinking our own thoughts and expressing our own individual identity, we take the risk of moving away from others. Therein lies a risk of loneliness.

The conflict between group pressure and personal values is often a central one for young people at this age, although some would argue that it continues to be a problem throughout life. No conflict is restricted totally to a particular age group, as anyone who has experienced a slice of life knows.

There are some factors that further complicate the issue, one being the different rates of maturation. The physical development of the adolescent has a great impact on self-image; the problem is that different individuals develop at markedly different rates and cultural expectations play a role in how young people are seen, and how they see themselves.

For example, boys who are late-maturing may experience stress and anxiety when they are treated as younger than they really are, while boys who mature early are more likely to develop a positive self-image because they are given more responsibility by adults and they are more likely to be regarded as leaders.

Girls are not immune here: girls who mature early may be embarrassed by their obvious femininity while girls who mature late may feel isolated from their girlfriends who are interested in some degree of sexual exploration.

The point is that adolescents are made more vulnerable by the timing of their growth pattern; depending on when it happens in relation to the rest of the group or the class, physical maturation, or the delay of it, can be an isolating experience.

An identity crisis

The self-esteem of adolescents often declines at around the age of twelve or thirteen before increasing gradually over the next few years. This could be due to a number of reasons, among them the physical upheaval that puberty brings, and the self-consciousness about changing body image. Another explanation is that at this time young people have moved from primary school and are now amongst the youngest and least competent in what can be a large, seemingly impersonal environment.

In arriving at a general description for the way that human beings develop socially and emotionally, psychologist Erik Erikson[1] considered the stages we pass through from birth to death. He suggested that we face what he called a 'psychosocial crisis' at each stage, a very specific conflict that defines the stage for us. He believed that the decline in self-esteem among adolescents was due to their re-evaluating themselves and their goals in their search for an identity.

It is now that a person begins to ask 'Who am I?' and 'Who will I be?' Contemplating on an ideal self and who they are now, they may recognise major discrepancies that would cause the way they feel about themselves to plummet.

However much in a rush a young person might be to answer these questions and to 'arrive', establishing a stable identity is a very gradual process. Some would argue that it can take a lifetime, but it seems that by about the age of twenty most people have some sense of identity with which to work and to step forward into the future. Putting an age to it could lead some to despair, but in the next chapter we will consider those who are much older than twenty years of age and who feel they are still in the process of searching for an identity.

Adolescence, then, is a time of questioning the self and the self-concept. Psychologists may talk of the need for 'mature identity statuses' as a prerequisite for truly intimate relationships, but here we will call it a strong sense of self together with a healthy self-concept.

FEELING LONELY
The effects of changes

In the light of all that is going on, it is not surprising that loneliness can be so intense during adolescence. A number of studies report great loneliness in young people, including one that involved 9000 adolescents aged between 10 and 18. It was estimated from the results that 10 to 15% of the adolescents were 'seriously lonely', while almost 45% experienced chronic loneliness that was not quite so severe.[2] More than half agreed with the statement 'I often feel lonely'.

Another study that involved 5000 young people from the United States, Australia and Ireland, reported that about 20% of young people aged between 12 and 16, and about 13% of those aged between 16 and 20, agreed that 'I am so very lonely'.[3]

The developmental changes we have considered are certainly a great contributing factor to the extent of loneliness in young people. The changes can be distressing, involving as they do the disruption of existing attachments: the deep emotional tie to parents needs to be transformed, and childhood ways need to make way for more adult-like behaviour. At the same time there is an increased need for closeness with peers.

It is during their children's adolescence that parents start to lose their status as the primary attachment figures, and relationships with friends, both platonic and sexual, gradually become more important. This process probably happens in fits and starts, with the young person dipping in and out of childhood dependencies and attachments.

Separation from the pre-adolescent identity can be as painful as separation from parents: the previous self-concept no longer fits, and there can be a real disruption in personal and social reference points. What is often overlooked is that adolescents spend some time in mourning both for their childhood identity and for what they believed in childhood and the associated attachments.

Fifteen-year-old Ben had this to say about growing up:

When I was about twelve I used to tell everyone I wanted to be a children's book writer. That way, I thought, I could hold on to my childhood and never leave it because I would be writing about the sorts of things I loved then and dreamed about.

It was strange letting go of all those fairytale things: I can still remember the shock of realising there was no Santa Claus or Tooth Fairy but still pretending I believed in them, partly to help my parents out because they wanted me to keep believing, and partly because I was afraid to let them go.

I think I've grown past all that now, but I still feel sad when I think of not being a child any more — I feel frightened of what it means to be grown up.

The consequences of separation

Robert Weiss, who has been mentioned already as initiating loneliness research, wrote about this particular stage that there are times when there is no attachment figure available and the world seems empty and unable to provide such a figure at all. 'The parents no longer serve in this way. Now it is possible to speak of loneliness as a condition of objectless pining, of pining for a kind of relationship rather than for a particular person.'[4]

The consequence of this may be a refuge in romance, with the belief and the hope that it will satisfy the pining that Weiss describes. Initially it may well do that, and the young lovers may feel for a time that they are now complete, experiencing what is not at all unlike the adult experience of romantic attachment that we will discuss later on.

However, while the young couple may find themselves attached to each other, the relationship may be based on the fear of isolation and loneliness. The belief here is that to have a partner is to be not alone and lonely. But when this belief is held, true 'individuation'[5] — the process of becoming an individual with a clearly defined self — hasn't quite finished, and so the couple will be unlikely to be relating in a genuinely intimate way.

What started off as a safe retreat and as a buffer to the outside world could finally lead to an increased sense of isolation because of the lack of genuine contact.

It has been suggested that the sense of separation from the family that confronts the adolescent at this time revives early fears of separation from the mother. Re-experiencing that original trauma may lead to an escape of some kind — if not a romantic attachment, then perhaps alcohol or drug use, which are just two examples of the range of behaviours that may be largely motivated by the need for peer acceptance and the drive to conform to the norms of the peer group.

Adolescents may see only two choices for themselves: to have identity with a group, or else to be alienated. Consequently there can be strong tension between the values of the individual and the family, and peer pressure to violate these values. In an attempt to assert personal independence, adolescents may resist parental values, although often this is temporary. However, for those adolescents not sure of their own worth, the possibility of peer rejection may be enough to violate quite important values. What began as harmless experimentation may become more serious and destructive.

The attraction of drugs is not hard to understand: the drug-induced state can give a sense of well-being, the individual abandons anxieties and tensions, and may seem to reach deep insight into complex issues. The experience can be very pleasurable, and it can be a means of escape from an unhappy personal world where loneliness is a common companion.

Heavy drug involvement, however, means that problems are avoided rather than met head-on. Doubts about the future, about friendships, about body image, about developing skills, about family relationships, are all part of the development of adolescents, and their resolution lays the groundwork for a healthy functioning self.

Taking responsibility

Assuming independence and autonomy means taking responsibility: this can be terrifying, to become the main decision-maker in one's life! So many choices, so many possibilities ... Feelings of confusion abound, as the young person has to rely more and more on personal resources.

Insecurity and a sense of aloneness are often consequences of premature independence which may be foisted on adolescents. At the other end of the scale, when the struggle for independence is undermined by parents who encourage further dependence in their children, loneliness is a common result. When the developing of a personal identity and the developing of social relationships with peers are thwarted or delayed, the individual can feel very much alone and alienated.

For many adolescents, but for lonely adolescents in particular, boredom is a very great problem. While parents structure children's time when they are younger, in adolescence there is not the same extent of parental control over the way they use their time, and, left to their own resources and their own need to take charge of their time, young people can become bored and aimless.

What helps here is finding outlets for the abilities, talents and interests that emerge during adolescence. These outlets may be causes, or values, or ideologies, or sports, whatever inspires enthusiasm and can provide something that is important and valued in the young person's life.

The next step is to participate in some way in giving expression to these outlets, in finding worthwhile involvement to affirm the young person's sense of commitment and to reinforce belongingness.

It is timely to ask ourselves whether we fail our youth when, as a society, we cannot provide adequate opportunities for them to use their talents to do anything of significance.

Limited numbers of jobs necessarily means limited opportunities, but even those jobs that are available are often menial and repetitive, with low intrinsic interest.

Young people want to feel they are involved in something meaningful and productive, as we all do, and that their talents and energies are appreciated and needed. When this does not happen, when opportunity for expression is denied, they can become discouraged, depressed and lonely. Not surprisingly, at least one study has found that those young people who were very lonely scored higher than others on their perception of blocked access to opportunities in the areas of education, occupation, and recreation.[6]

Our culture's failure to transmit a sense of purpose or meaning to our young people can lead to teenage suicide. When there is little or no emotional support available, the ability to cope with setbacks or personal difficulties is limited; accordingly, resistance to feelings of despair is weakened, and suicide may seem the only option.

Adolescent suicide crosses all social classes, and has been dubbed 'the equal opportunity tragedy'; suicide rates among the young no longer lag well behind those for adults. Whatever the age of the individual, suicide seems the ultimate act of alienation and loneliness. However, while obviously lonely people are most at risk here, sometimes those who are outwardly vital and seem socially involved can become suicidal. A social persona can hide a lonely, isolated soul.

It is up to all of us to try to read the signs: when we work on deeper levels of contact and understanding we have a better chance of recognising someone who is in need of help.

Social factors

All of us grow up and develop in the context of society, and so social and cultural factors have a large part to play in this process of development, including the alienation and loneliness that many adolescents experience.

To begin with, young people at this age often feel that

they enjoy no status, having neither the privileges nor special treatment of the child nor the advantages and total independence of the adult. Because our society has no firm and structured 'rites of passage' for a child moving into adolescence, they can feel neither one thing nor another, deprived as yet of any true social role.

Whether they like it or not, school forms a large part of their lives, even in terms of the time required to be there. The important place that competition holds at school — either in the classroom or on the sports field — can make those who continually fail to achieve there feel inadequate, and consequently rejected and isolated.

Added to all this, there are strong pressures to have friends, to be popular, to be 'good-looking', to be successful. These expectations come from all quarters: parents, teachers, peers, and, not least, from the mass media. Unrealistic and extreme as they are, these expectations bring enormous pressure to bear on young people, and for those who fail to measure up in some way, feelings of inadequacy lurk and prey. As one fourteen-year-old girl put it:

> I know it's stupid of me, but it does worry me that I don't look like some girls on TV, even though I don't say anything to my friends. I can talk to Mum about it, and she tells me that I'm lovely, intelligent, delightful — all the things that mums say to their kids — and that's comforting, but sometimes I feel as if other people are looking at me and comparing me unfavourably with those soapie stars.

The self-consciousness that this girl reveals is not uncommon among teenagers. It is most usually the response to the various problems of adolescence, notably the process of disruption and then reorganising of the self-concept. The need to build identity, to win peer approval and acceptance, to establish independence and to find some significance in a social role, can lead to a good deal of self-preoccupation which, as we will see, can have many positive aspects.

The fact that this girl can talk to her mother about the things that worry her, and that her mother can offer support and reassurance, is fortunate for her. We must never underestimate the role of supportive, interested, nurturing and encouraging parents and other adults, including teachers: they provide the bridge for adolescents to pass over into the adult world with a more sure and confident step than they might otherwise have.

The family scene

The full extent of support is not always available, especially with the current variation in family structures. Increased rates of divorce and separation, single-parent homes, two working parents, the blended family, the demise of the nuclear family on the heels of the demise of the extended family — all these have been blamed for the loneliness and sense of alienation and isolation in children and adolescence.

Like human beings, society is a dynamic thing and so involves change: rather than trying to turn the tide we would do better to work on our individual selves, putting effort into maintaining our personal values and supporting others in doing the same.

Disintegration of any highly valued system is painful: it signals loss of structure, and, along with that, a loss of direction and meaning. It takes strong individuals to push on effectively, and where we are in positions to influence the young, we have a particular responsibility.

Certainly, for children and young people alike, good role models are essential. As we discussed earlier, for example, a young child learns how to deal with feelings like anger through witnessing an older person expressing them appropriately, cleanly and openly and with no blame or other destructive behaviour. By observation, children and adolescents learn ways of handling conflict and the ultimate pleasures of effective resolution.

Because, as they are developing, adolescents are being

confronted with many disruptions to usual patterns — the ways of relating to parents, for example, or changes in self-concept that accompany the emergence from childhood — further disruptions, such as family break-up, make life rather more complicated.

Whatever the circumstances surrounding parental break-up, the likelihood is that both parents are faced with many issues to resolve. How they go about doing this can provide good role modelling for their children, but all the same their emotional resources are probably taken up with their own need to rearrange and reintegrate their priorities. Because of this, their children may suffer, even temporarily, from lack of warmth, protection, support, affirmation and guidance. Aware and conscious parents will make an effort to supply these when they can.

When the break-up is bitter, the children are likely to suffer much more: not only do they have to readjust to a new family structure, but they also witness acrimony between two people important in their lives.

Beth is now twenty-two years old, but she recalls the time surrounding her parents' separation when she was sixteen:

> It wasn't so much that they were breaking up that was awful — lots of people in my class at school, and most of my friends, just lived with one parent after their parents split, so it probably wasn't as big a deal as it used to be.
>
> Of course I wished they could have stayed together — what kids wouldn't? My sister and I used to make secret bets that they would fall in love again after they were apart for a while, but that was just us wishing and hoping that we could all be together again, the way we were when we were little.
>
> The worst thing, though, was that they hated each other in the end. After Dad moved out there were all these terrible phone calls back and forth — Mum would be screaming abuse at him and Dad would be yelling

down the phone too. I hated it. Dad wanted us girls to be with him, and he even asked us once if we wouldn't prefer to be with him. I still feel that painful wrench in my heart when I remember him asking and the look in his eyes — he couldn't bear to leave us.

Notice that Beth and her sister wanted things to be the way they were when they were young — while this is a common feeling in adolescence, it is intensified when the family unit is coming apart. And note, too, that it wasn't the break-up itself that was so distressing, as the bitter and enraged expression of feelings between her parents.

Blending families takes particular skill, especially when adolescents are involved, because they are already in the process of restructuring their self-concept and becoming part of a new grouping can magnify the disruption. Again, aware and conscious adults will take this into account and try to provide as nurturing and supportive an atmosphere as possible.

When we are considering the effects of changes — such as in the emerging pattern of family structures — we need to look beyond the changes themselves to pinpoint the source of the real distress. Family break-up may be inevitable, as we are now being told, but the effects on the individuals can be ameliorated. As one psychologist tells us:

> So much of the family's survival, together or separated, depends on the parents' determination to put parenting before hurt pride and to work together today to give their kids a reasonable and well-adjusted tomorrow ... Regardless of parents' crises the children biologically had two parents and most want to get on well with both. It's their fundamental right not to be asked to take sides, not to be used as an adult substitute, or in any other way be deprived of the fun, freedom and friendships that go with being young. If parents are lonely they must learn to lean on someone their own size.[7]

Personality and loneliness

Developmental and social changes can contribute very much to the loneliness of adolescence, as we've seen. Personal characteristics can increase the likelihood of loneliness that much more: they can determine whether or not an individual can get a friendship going and then maintain it, or whether they can cope, or even excel, in social situations.

Parents often worry that their adolescents aren't developing properly in some aspect. If they could be less lazy, more enthusiastic, less emotional, more sociable ... they would be happy adults, with lots of friends and a good job, and parents could take a bow for a job well done.

Certainly there are some qualities in our children that we would like to encourage, or bury — the fact is that they are who they are, and the best we can do is to accept them, to help them come to terms with themselves and enjoy who they are, and support them in changing those aspects of themselves that don't work for them.

In Chapter Two we looked at 'lonely types', and the lonely type of adolescent is not much different. They approach adolescence in the same way that a lonely adult might approach a challenge: with feelings of insecurity and anxiety and fears of rejection and alienation by others. They also tend to suffer from low self-esteem and the accompanying tendency to withdraw from other people which tends, in turn, to increase their sense of isolation.

All of these characteristics are observable in adults as well as in adolescents, but what is unique for the adolescent is the accompanying change in terms of development and social position. What tends to be more common in adolescence, too, is some long-term brooding.

On a more hopeful note adolescents do experience a drop in self-consciousness when they spend time alone and they benefit greatly afterwards in terms of a more positive emotional state. And those adolescents who spend more time alone tend to have more personal direction in their lives and a stronger sense of purpose.

The introspective nature of adolescence may appear to be an indulgence in self-preoccupation, but it can actually have a functional purpose: it could be seen as an opportunity to explore, clarify and understand what is happening, and to reach some insights into a range of aspects — relationships, identity and loneliness, for example. To withdraw from others for a while in this way can expand the capacity to be alone and give the chance to experience the positive aspects of solitude.

Adulthood

6

YOUNG ADULTHOOD
Self-image and maturity

Adolescence is the bridge between childhood and maturity, a time when we work at establishing a basic identity with which to make the major transition into adulthood. Who we take into adulthood as our 'self' depends on what has gone before. Our history largely, though not entirely, determines our future.

During childhood we practised at being grown-up through role-playing. Some of us tried out very many roles, imagining through fantasy what it felt like to be this character or that. Even comic and cartoon characters with their fantastical escapades were fodder for our fertile young imaginations.

For those of us not so keen on extensive role-playing, the few roles we did play out were enough to give us a taste of being what could be called 'other'. It helped lay a foundation for choice later on, even though that choice may have been relatively limited.

During adolescence we continued to role-play but in a different sense. We were the friend, the confidant, the daughter or the son, sister or brother, the student, the neighbour, the horse-rider or the young scientist, the marvellous movie-buff or the skilled skate-board rider. The roles involved more serious consideration: we were no longer pretending but were now making choices about the things we liked to do, the people we liked to be with, and the sort of person we wanted to be.

This ideal self — the person we wanted to be — sometimes seemed a long way off from the way we were. Consequently, our self-esteem could suffer terribly, depending on the extent of the discrepancy between what we viewed as the ideal and what we viewed as the reality.

Many of us might remember the words of encouragement from parents or other relatives or teachers to the effect that we must not undervalue ourselves. What they saw then was our tendency to disregard our worth and to underestimate our capacity.

What may have been playing in our minds was the movie featuring the ideal self, the one who was all-powerful, all-popular, all-competent and all-admired. Little wonder that the reality was a disappointment.

Did we move from adolescence into adulthood disillusioned with ourselves? If we did, chances are that our self-concept continued to be poor and ragged for at least some time.

For those of us who see ourselves in a negative light, life can be very lonely. Coming from this perspective, we tend to see others in one of two ways: either we feel they have succeeded where we have not, in which case the gulf between our perceived achievements and consequent value keeps us apart, or else we feel that others are no better than we are, in which case, because we think poorly of ourselves, we don't think any better of those others around us.

If, however, we emerged from adolescence with a healthy self-image, if we felt that life was a challenge while acknowledging some normal apprehension about the future, then we would have been off to a more solid start in our maturing process.

Psychosocial theory often tells us that we become adult at twenty years of age or thereabouts, and the consensus of our society is that people should be standing more or less 'on their own two feet' by this time. 'The worst thing about turning twenty was that I felt as if I had to be adult all the time now,' said one student. 'When you are in your teens people excuse you for more because you are a teenager and not grown-up yet. But reach twenty and there is no excuse.'

It is usually around this time that young people are moving towards an occupational goal and making plans for their future. It seems an obvious cut-off point from other angles too: schooling has well and truly ended and the earlier strong ties with home and parents are losing their pull.

But while we may be called — and call ourselves — 'young adults', we have not made a magical leap into sudden maturity. Adulthood and maturity, while closely interrelated, are not synonymous terms: adulthood means a certain stage of life which lasts many years and sees many aspects of living. Maturity is something we attain along the way, learning from our life experiences while expanding our store of wisdom.

On emerging from our years of adolescence, many of us feel alone and frightened rather than excited and even exhilarated about the possibilities for tomorrow. There are many possible reasons for feeling this way but one of them is that we see adulthood as a burden, a state requiring instant maturity for responsible and wise decision-making.

But we need to recognise that life is a continuing maturation process and that, while we may reach milestones along the way, individuals differ vastly in just when they reach those milestones.

Who am I now?

It is assumed that, by the time we reach our early twenties, we have some sense of personal identity, some sort of answer to that question of questions — 'Who am I?' Most of us do. Whether we stretch the boundaries of that identity during our lifetime is another matter.

The essence of who we are stands firm and unassailable: how we function in the world, how we work and how we play, bears our ineffable mark, our essence. But our identity is multi-faceted, composed of many aspects of ourselves, and in answering truly 'Who am I?' we refer to many dimensions of ourselves.

Our capacity for change expands the possibilities for identity even further: to grow as a human being inevitably involves change of some kind so that the 'I' of our early adult years may be a significantly changed 'I' by our middle or later adult years. For this reason, the identity with which we emerge after adolescence could be called a provisional identity. All the same, our essence, which belongs to the spiritual domain, remains unchanged.

So, from adolescence we move from a state of some confusion as to who we are to a state of some stability with the establishing of an identity that is ours. Erikson believed that during the time between about twelve and twenty years of age the conflict revolves around our identity and role confusion, and on grappling with the question 'Who am I?' and coming to terms with it, we move on to our next stage, the stage of young adulthood when the crisis involves intimacy as opposed to isolation.

At this stage, he believed, we have a drive to form strong friendships and to establish an intimate relationship with a significant other person in our life. Not satisfying this drive towards relationship, Erikson warned, could lead to feelings of loneliness. He wrote: 'In youth you find out what you care to do and who you care to be — even in changing roles. In young adulthood you learn whom you care to be with — at work and in private life.'[1] In this way, he went on, we do not only exchange intimacies, but we also share intimacy.

Getting down to serious business

For most of us, relationships are central to our existence as human beings who are living in a society. At work, at home and at play we interact with others and usually establish some sort of relationship with at least a few others in our lives, whatever our age. However solitary an existence we choose later on, our early years are most usually marked by the presence of other people.

During childhood and adolescence, as we've seen, interactions with our peers are essential in expanding our world-view. As infants and young children we are necessarily egocentric — our survival depends on it — and interacting with others gives us a wider perspective with regard to other people. The skills we learn in relating to others accumulate so that, by the time we have reached late adolescence, we are somewhat ready for the more serious business of relating.

While the whole area of relationships becomes important during early adulthood, this is not to say that intimacy and becoming attached to others belong solely to this time of life. Some people learn to be truly intimate only when they seem to be verging on old age, if not beyond. Nor do we all wait until we are a particular age before embarking on a serious relationship: there are fifteen-year-olds who relate more genuinely and lovingly to each other and with more understanding than people who are much, much older.

But it is generally at the end of adolescence and in those early years of being an adult in the eyes of the world that relationships, and particularly those with a significant other person, become a real focus.

Because of the many aspects of relationships, and because of the fact that they are so central to our lives, a whole chapter is devoted to them later on.

Making choices

Rules are more relaxed these days regarding the choices we make about our future in young adulthood. While once the norm was that we would settle down, have kids, and give time to a career (especially if we were male), the ground rules now are different.

Our options have expanded — for both males and females — so that for those of us prepared to risk being different we are not totally without support as we once might have been. But while expanded options make life easier in some ways, they can also bring with them the complexity of choice. Where once we might have followed a well-trodden path, with our futures fairly well mapped out in advance, we now have very many possible paths before us.

What does this mean for us? For those of us feeling unsure about ourselves, the multiplicity of choices can be overwhelming and even immobilising. They can leave us feeling even more unsure and frightened, alone in a confusing and demanding world.

We might be pressured by others in our life — parents, partners, other relatives, employers, friends — to follow certain paths and, out of fear and uncertainty about ourselves, we might embark on one that does not particularly speak to us. Or, as a reaction against such pressure, we might walk a road that others would never have believed we would choose.

Whatever we decide to do in our young adulthood, the true and long-term impact is felt later when we move further into adulthood, taking our histories and our choices with us.

MIDDLE ADULTHOOD
The challenge

If the main task of adolescence is to establish identity, and the main task of young adulthood is to establish relationships and an occupational future, then the main task of middle adulthood is to direct one's own life and to shape the lives of others too.

We are talking here in terms of Erikson's psychosocial crises, where each stage of life presents us with a basic conflict to resolve before we move on to the next stage. According to this view, the ability to be intimate which we develop during young adulthood requires that we have an identity, which we have developed during adolescence. And the ability to reach out to others and to care about improving the world in general depends on the extent to which we can love and be intimate with specific others in our lives.

We have to remember that theories provide us with a framework to help us conceptualise what is happening, but they are not perfect descriptions of reality. For example, there are exceptions to this theory: there are those for whom intimacy is too difficult and who have no close, significant others in their lives, and yet they give generously of their resources to provide a better way of life for others in society. These people are often, although not always, lonely for human companionship and closeness, but they choose to sublimate their deep feelings and to help others.

For most of us, though, middle adulthood presents a continuing opportunity to expand certain skills. At work, at home and in child rearing, we are becoming more and more sensitive to the many needs of those around us.

Because what we are calling middle adulthood stretches between the ages of about thirty-five and sixty-five, it covers a vast range of experiences involving work and home. Young children develop into adolescents and then into young adults who eventually leave home during the space of this time; people move through the ranks at work to arrive at, or to miss out on, a coveted position; parents of people in this age bracket are ageing and often require at least some care and attention.

This is indeed a time of challenge and often one challenge after another or even, quite commonly, one on top of another. We require all our resources to deal with them and to cope effectively.

By and large, our style of life has been established early in adulthood: the pace of our living, the way we balance work and leisure, the setting up of a group of friends with whom we share differing degrees of closeness, and our choice of activities which are a reflection of our values and our interests.

During middle adulthood we usually continue in this style unless some life event confronts us with a need for change: separation from a partner and the end of a relationship, or retrenchment from a position held for many years, or a serious financial crisis of some sort.

The event that is the catalyst for change may not necessarily be so catastrophic or momentous by others' standards: but usually in this case the potential and desire for change has been bubbling away, waiting for an opportunity to make itself known.

Life events

During middle adulthood we experience more life events than perhaps at any other time in our lives. Committing ourselves to a partnership in a continuing way, managing the crises in our children's lives, changing jobs, being promoted or being retrenched, separating from a partner, friends' relationships unravelling, losing someone close, parents becoming dependent, our children leaving home ... We respond in our individual ways to all of these different events.

Many such events involve some degree of loss: it may be loss of a person or persons in our lives, it may be loss of a type of lifestyle, it may be loss of freedom or independence or autonomy. What accompanies such loss may be feelings of marginality, or feelings of confusion and self-doubt can settle in, chewing away at any confidence that may be left.

Where the loss involves a person close to us, feelings of attachment persist, whatever the circumstances of loss. These can be very confusing when they coexist with feelings of bitterness or hostility towards, for example, a rejecting or abandoning partner. And they can be very distressing in the case of bereavement, where the bereaved person needs to come to terms with the physical and emotional loss of an intimate person in their lives.

Losing someone close to us can deal a devastating blow. Losing a partner, especially when the relationship was rich and satisfying, can be particularly difficult because the principal sharer is no longer there. 'When Rob died,' says one widow, 'I felt lonely beyond belief. We were both young — in our thirties — and I was devastated that I had lost not only my partner, but the wonderful future we had planned together. I had many friends, but he was my closest friend and the father of my children.'

It isn't only when the relationship has been good that loneliness strikes. One recently divorced woman commented on the deep loneliness she has felt over the last eighteen months since the split. 'I thought I would feel blessed relief once it was finished. Instead I felt this overwhelming loneliness, and it's only now that I am coming to terms with it.' Any sort of loss results in grieving. At this time, more than at any other, we are forced into the awareness that we are fundamentally alone. It is possible that the woman who experienced loneliness rather than the expected relief after separation and divorce after a tumultuous relationship was dealing with this confronting aspect of grief.

All life events involve a transitional period during which we can feel very alone in the world: the associated change means an adjustment to a new way of living, or a new way of being, and while others can offer support at this time, we need to muster the resources ourselves to manage the change in an ultimately satisfying way.

Some events in our lives herald deep change of a sort we may not have imagined. Take this example.

Karin is a woman of about forty-five whose two children have recently left home. These 'children' are twenty-three and twenty-one, and their moving out together had been planned for some time. Both Karin and her husband Ross were quite looking forward to a quieter house and more time together, although because their children spend a lot of time out, they had been enjoying these things for some time. Karin says:

> It was a funny feeling. I thought I was absolutely prepared for it, but when they finally left, and even though they were returning the next week for a dinner together with us, I felt this great sadness.
>
> It isn't as if I've devoted myself totally to motherhood — I enjoy teaching and I want to continue with that — but I did feel at the time that somehow I had no purpose any more. How melodramatic this sounds! But really, I had to admit to myself how much being a mother means to me and how much energy I'd put into that role over those many years.
>
> I was talking to Ross about all this, and what suddenly struck me was that we all limit ourselves so much when we think about our roles. For example, I enjoy being a mother to my kids, and I always will, and, who knows, I might even be a grandparent one day too, and I would love that. But ... why stop at parenting my own children? Heaven knows that I put energy and care into my students at school — that's parenting too, in a way.
>
> So, suddenly, I feel I have this new lease on life. I can continue to parent actively on a day-to-day basis, even though my own children are out on their own. I thank them for teaching me so much about being a parent, and I put all the learning to good use!

Karin's story illustrates how events in our lives can lead us to deeper understanding about ourselves and those around us, and also how we can begin to turn our attentions to a wider circle as we grow older, offering wisdom and care to those beyond our immediate relatives, friends and acquaintances.

Parenting

Karin's comment about the generality of parenting is an interesting one. Here is someone who has taken the skills of parenting into a wider sphere, applying what she has learned to others who are in need of parenting.

Who is in need of parenting? All of us at different times. It isn't just the obviously abandoned or the obviously damaged who require this kind of loving and caring and nurturing, but all of us.

Clarissa Pinkola Estés reminds us that even if we had the best mother in the world, we may have more than one eventually. She has often told her own daughters:

> You are born to one mother, but if you are lucky, you will have more than one. And among them all you will find most of what you need. Your relationships with ... the many mothers will most likely be ongoing ones, for the need for guidance and advisement is never outgrown ...[2]

During actual parenting, we will sometimes be acutely aware of our own history of being parented: by parenting our own children we may subconsciously re-create situations similar to our own, or we may consciously try to make things different. What we may do at the same time is to treat the inner parent and the inner child that each of us has.

This is an important concept for the treatment of loneliness, especially in the context of separation anxiety. If loneliness is, indeed, linked to such anxiety as is originally experienced in infancy, then perhaps we can be our own parent in reassuring our frightened inner child and in keeping it company.

The grand reassessment

Too often, the restlessness and frustration, the unhappiness and the anguish that may be expressed later on in life, when the challenges and crises of early adulthood have been met and resolved and are finished with, are put down to the passing of youth.

This syndrome has been tagged 'the mid-life crisis', and all manner of actions and reactions have been put down to it. Personally I prefer the term 'the second journey'[3] for the experience, rather than 'mid-life crisis', partly because it replaces the concept of crisis with a more exciting possibility — a journey has more interesting implications. As well, a journey means that we are participating in what we experience, moving along with it, rather than remaining helpless victims at the hands of a cruel crisis.

In describing the different nature of this journey, Carl Jung warned us of taking the truths and ideals that have worked for us until this point into the next phase of our lives. He had this to say: '... we cannot live the afternoon of life according to the programme of life's morning: for what in the morning was true will at evening have become a lie.'[4]

A second journey can be excruciatingly lonely. It can even be initiated by the recognition that ultimately we are all alone, and we can bind no other to us. It requires deep soul-searching and careful decision-making.

In his book *The Second Journey*, Gerald O'Collins points out that these journeys may end in one of two ways: either the individual reaches a new place and a new commitment, or else they go back to where they originally were, but they reaffirm the old place and the old commitment in a new way. How do we choose between the alternatives?

Jan and Robert, a couple in their late forties, have faced a major reassessment of their lives, a second journey for them both. What seemed to set it off were two events: after a long illness which involved a good deal of Jan's time, her mother died, and at around the same time, Robert was passed over for his last chance at a promotion in his job.

> I would have thought that I was prepared for Mum's death, and in some ways it was a blessed relief — she was terribly ill towards the end — but I seemed to fall apart afterwards. Of course I realise that while she was alive I

had to keep going, never giving in to all the fatigue and the emotional cost too. I visited her very often, and tried to keep her spirits up, and I tried to do the same for the rest of the family too — staying cheerful, telling them we had to keep looking ahead, that sort of thing.

When Mum died, what was like this enormous facade came tumbling down. I was in a terrible way for some time, and only a small part of it was really grief for Mum, because I had done a lot of grieving for her already when she was dying.

The grieving seemed to be for something else. Part of me didn't know what to do with myself, even though I work and I am very involved with what I do. It was a feeling of being lost and unsure of myself. I felt alone, too, because Robert was so caught up with his work and with trying to sort things out for himself.

He and I have had to do a lot of thinking, and we've spent some time apart trying to sort things out for ourselves. I don't know how things will end at the moment.

Robert takes up their story:

It has been an awful time for both of us. Jan has tried to be supportive I suppose but she's been trying to come to terms with things too.

For a brief time, after this promotion thing happened — or didn't happen, as it turned out! — I was involved with a woman at work. She had just separated from her husband and was going through a rough time. It was not a wise thing to do, partly because she started to get emotionally involved, but it did help my self-esteem a bit. I have been feeling terribly alone, and sometimes there doesn't seem to be any way out. Jan talks to her girlfriends about it, and that helps her, but who can I talk to if Jan shuts down with me?

Jan and Robert's story reveals the sorts of events — or crises — that can launch people onto their second journey. Robert's missing out on what he sees as the last chance for promotion amounted to failure for him. If he anticipated reaching a certain goal by a certain age, where to now?

His one intimate companion, Jan, was trying to come to terms with her own challenges at this time, conscious of Robert's being unavailable to help her. At the same time, Robert felt left on his own to deal with what amounted to a devastating blow.

Traditionally, women have been the ones to put effort into friendships and relationships in general, as Jan has done. They often enjoy a network of friends that men of Robert's generation may not have. Feeling isolated, Robert turned to someone he could help in some way. Perhaps he was projecting the help he needed for himself onto someone else, a common ploy when we just don't know how else to comfort ourselves.

This is a difficult time for Jan and Robert. As Gerald O'Collins writes: '... we must let go if we are to be broken up, remade and restructured. Our world suddenly comes apart at the seams. We cannot mend it. Let it come apart — even at the cost of much pain.'[5]

Not everyone embarks on a second journey, nor are second journeys the same for any two people. The same sorts of events or situations may precipitate them, but how we experience what comes afterwards, what meaning we take from them, and how we choose to live our lives as a result, are very individual.

THE LATER YEARS
A last journey

I like the description of this time of life by Malcolm Muggeridge, who likens himself to a man on a sea voyage that is coming to its final destination. Notice, again, the sense of journey: 'When I embarked I worried about having a cabin with a porthole, whether I should be asked to sit at the Captain's table, who were the more attractive and important passengers. All such considerations become pointless when I shall so soon be disembarking ...'[6]

The later years may involve some particular events: retirement from a job, moving into a smaller home or unit, or a retirement or nursing home, or the death of a spouse. During these years older people may lose not only a spouse, but also old friends, other relatives, and work colleagues.

It is inevitable that we will experience aloneness to some extent as we grow older. But does it need to be a sign of social failure? Or of loneliness? After all, being alone can also bring with it independence and a degree of autonomy. All the same, companionship can be a precious commodity, and being involved with other people, as well as receiving care from others, is desirable for people of all ages, but especially when we are aged.

Widowed — the self as a first resource

Women are most likely to be widowed at this time, but despite the great sense of loss and aloneness that bereavement brings, it doesn't necessarily mark the end of social involvement. All the same, to lose someone to whom we feel important can be devastating, and especially if we feel that no-one else considers us to be important.

There are a number of levels and forms that loneliness can take for widows.[7] They experience loneliness in the here and now, and they can also feel nostalgia for past days: here the feelings of loneliness are relative, not as far as others are concerned, but with respect to the old days, when the partner was alive and well and life ran smoothly. Widows may also feel a 'loneliness anxiety' for the days ahead with no loved one or companion under the same roof. Here is a variety of feeling-states all associated with the experience of loneliness. As one group of writers says, loneliness is more likely to occur because of the great stress on the importance of marriage in our society and on the importance of the couple relationship. 'Loneliness can be experienced in terms of a specific other person who is no longer available as a love object (or even a hate object) even when other social and emotionally supportive relations are part of the support systems of a person.'[8]

The same writers point out that studies reveal that, on being asked how they cope with their loneliness, many widows reveal that they regard the 'self' as a first resource. It is the self that keeps intact the great store of memories that can be dipped into at will, and the self that can put the situation into perspective.

The extent of personal resources that widows may have varies enormously: the more education a person has, the greater the personal resources tend to be. The more likely, too, are various complex and satisfying networks that can offer both emotional and social support.

It is worth noting that many women report enjoying a new-found independence in widowhood: what they discover are the joys of self-sufficiency, and more freedom than they have experienced before. This is not to underestimate the pain of bereavement, but it can give hope to those who are currently bereaved, a hope for opportunities in the future and the possibility of a happy life despite a sad loss.

Old and alone?

Increased longevity and lower birth rates have meant that the proportion of people in the older age bracket has increased dramatically, and will continue to increase. It seems, too, that the older age group is comprised mainly of widowed women.

Very few older people live in institutions, in spite of the myths, with most living either on their own — especially those who are widowed — or with one other person, usually a spouse. It would seem, then, that to be old most usually means being alone. This status is belonging to more and more people, in particular older, widowed women.

Does 'being alone' for these people also mean 'being

lonely'? In terms of stereotype, the prevailing notion is that to be old means to be lonely because of being alone: old people are often seen to be unwanted by their families and to have no close relationships or social contacts.

While this may hold true for some, it does not seem to describe the situation for many older people, who report regular contact with relatives and especially their adult children. It does seem that expectations have a large part to play here: older people who accept that their children have lives of their own and keep loving contact with them rather than making demands and passing judgement often report less loneliness.

Why might this be? Perhaps because, in accepting that others' lives are separate and worthwhile they are affirming their own lives, and in keeping loving contact with their children they are practising keeping loving contact with others too. On the other hand, unmet expectations can be a source of great unhappiness and loneliness. In some situations, having no expectations at all, while putting effort into a satisfying life, can hold most rewards.

A few studies[9] from some years ago have indicated that for older people it was contact with friends and neighbours that had more impact on their well-being than did contact with either their children or other relatives. It could be that some fifteen or twenty years later this is still the case. As one social worker has pointed out:

> Older people may think that it would be just wonderful to live with their adult children, but these days with everyone going out to work all day, the older person can feel very isolated. They really do need to be with other people with the same time-frame and with similar interests and outlook on life.

Feeling in control
Helplessness and hopelessness are the common outcomes of feeling that things are out of control. On the other hand, feeling in control of a situation can reduce stress considerably.

The significance here for older people is that certain life events can leave them feeling that they have no control over their lives: forced retirement, for example, or the death of their friends or their relatives, or a decline in their health, can all leave an older person feeling lost, confused and not in control.

Older people feel it is not easy to establish new friendships easily, in contrast to young people who tend to find it easier. As well, while for the young separation from friends and family usually means a move into the future, for the old it is most usually because others move away or because the older person becomes housebound or is ill and needs hospitalisation. Losing control of a pattern of life can be a serious problem of ageing especially if we are forced to be alone when we would rather be in company.

To demonstrate the important part that control plays in social contact, one study involved students visiting residents of a retirement home over an eight-week period. The results were fascinating: those residents who could choose when and how long these visits would be reported themselves to be happier, more hopeful and less lonely than those residents whose visitors came by unpredictably, even though the actual visiting time was about the same.

The forces of age may seem to involve a loss of personal control and to lead ageing people on a path of powerlessness and isolation. However, there is a need to challenge the belief that loneliness and loss of such control are inevitable with advancing years: this belief in such inevitability can be a self-fulfilling prophecy. On the other hand there are many people who live satisfying and fulfilled lives throughout this time. The Director of Nursing of a nursing home says this:

> We have a wide range of people here, in terms of how dependent they are and in terms of outlook on life too. There are one or two in particular who, although they are confined to wheelchairs and have had traumatic and chaotic physical experiences, still reach out to the others,

comforting them and reassuring them, even though those others may be physically better off. There is little else they can have control over in their lives, but they depend on their own good-will and their own ability to give some nurturance to others. It gives them a sense of personal power.

Redirecting energy

Introspection may have been a hallmark of adolescence, but it makes a reappearance during older age if it hasn't before. It is now that we reflect on our life and all the events and people and experiences that have contributed to it. Such introspection is vital for a satisfactory integration. As Carl Jung wrote: 'For a young person it is almost a sin ... to be too pre-occupied with himself; but for the ageing person it is a duty and a necessity to devote serious attention to himself.'[10]

Now is the time for good old reminiscence, which has more than sentimental value: reminiscing allows us to pull the essential threads of our lives together into a meaningful tapestry and to understand the evolving of our values and beliefs and outlooks through various life events.

Reminiscing is therapeutic, especially for bereaved and lonely older people who are trying to regain some control and direction in their lives. It encourages them to remember a time when life was good and the richness of those times can sustain them now. Our own child is still part of us, just as the unsure teenager and the cocky young adult are. Reminiscing is a way of contacting those parts of ourselves and introducing one to the other. It is a whole-being integration of sorts.

It has value, too, in creating a sense of continuity to our children and grandchildren, giving them a feeling of their own history through the tales of our experiences. In this way we reinforce our own self-worth, by telling stories of survival against all odds, of rising above difficult circumstances, of battling invisible foes to win in the end, of surrender and forgiveness and great wisdom. Reminiscence offers a true life confirmation.

At this time, we can look to new roles for ourselves: the role of grandparent requires all the skill and patience that parenting did, and with it can come a sense of renewal; on retirement, leisure activities can involve a significant investment of time, giving the older adult a whole new orientation; and community interests, which offer the opportunity to share our knowledge and our care beyond the family and ourselves, can give a new lease of life. All of these roles often require adaptation to some extent, which in itself indicates continuing growth for the older person rather than stagnation and decline.

The roles also provide a buffer against the isolation that we may experience in our older age. We may lose some of our independence, especially through illness, but we need not lose our capacity for involvement.

Face-to-face with mortality

At some stage in our lives we become fully aware of the fact that we have lived many, many more years than we can expect to live in the future. Now is often the time to review accomplishments, and to reflect on our earlier goals which, however positive an outlook we may have, are unlikely to be fulfilled.

This can be a discouraging time, but how we view our lives at this time is very much a reflection of how we have always tended to operate. In other words, if we can accept the 'failures' as part of being human and alive, and concentrate on what has been good and satisfying, we are more likely to feel confident about where we have been, what we have done and whom we have touched.

To accept our lives as they have been and to see them as part of a larger order is to see value in our own existence. This is a fine preparation for contemplation of our own death.

Many of us lose someone to death during earlier stages of

life, but it is during old age that we see more of our friends and relatives dying. The circumstances of the deaths can be distressing: long, painful illnesses take their time with one, and sudden, senseless death falls on another. How, I might wonder, will I die?

Facing death, whether or not it is impending, is probably the most solitary thing we ever do. People may gather at our bedside, may grieve over the imminent loss, but finally we die alone. It has been suggested, in fact, that the loneliness we experience throughout life is a precursor to this: we are aware of our essential aloneness and cry over what we believe to be our final isolation. Is this the reason that so many cultures of the world continue to fear the circumstances surrounding death?

Final separation it may be for some, but for those who embrace a spiritual dimension, physical death represents the next step in a journey. For others it is yet another event, albeit the last, and coming to terms with it is the final difficult challenge.

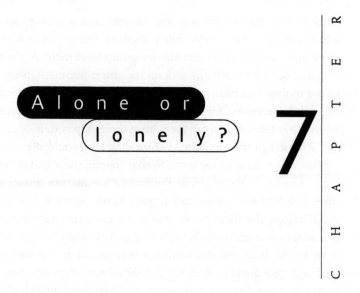

CHAPTER 7

Alone or lonely?

BEING ALONE
Our cultural bias

Togetherness is highly valued in most human societies. In the context of survival it makes perfect sense: working on the principle of one for all and all for one, the health and protection of the individual and of the group is assured.

Most preliterate societies are very wary of aloneness, with, for example, the fear of possible sorcery keeping people together in many of the African societies. Aloneness for short spurts of time in order to hunt or to gather is accepted as necessary for survival but any longer and suspicions and fear are aroused: for the Dobu, for example, to be alone means to be plotting against other tribe members.

While cultures such as these may have different ideas about loneliness from those that we have, their attitudes towards the state of aloneness are not so very different.

Preliterate societies certainly regard themselves in terms of the group, with little if any sense of individuality as we know it, the main priority being the welfare of the group as a whole. In fact, there have been societies where individuals were not welcome to remain as group members if their situation led to their being a drain on group resources. Some of the indigenous North American tribes of the past followed this principle when, for example, a male member died — his widow was expected to fall away from the group and, all alone and exposed to the elements, before long she would die.

But it is not only for survival that togetherness is held in high regard: the happiness of the individual and the group is often believed to be predicated upon being together. We are social beings, the theory goes, and so we need companionship and affection from other human beings from the time we are born to the time we die. Intimacy is regarded as a treasured goal and the quality of interpersonal relationships has been under scrutiny for some time for signs of how intimacy is developed between individuals.

Because of the accepted belief that togetherness is something to strive for and to maintain, being alone is seen as an unhappy and unfortunate state and to be avoided at all costs. Keeping busy, particularly in seeking out companionship, is the lot of many who find themselves solitary.

We are all familiar with the stereotype of the individual who lives alone: friendless and unfriendly, aloof and disinterested, unattractive and unapproachable, alone and lonely. The stereotypes go so far that sometimes those who are researching the subject of loneliness look to whether or not people are partnered to determine whether or not they are lonely: widowed, divorced and never-married individuals have been assumed to be the perfect subject — having a partner is regarded as a safeguard against loneliness.

Outdated as this attitude may seem, it is still more widespread than many of us might believe. The belief works two ways: often 'singles' will assume that any feelings of loneliness that they experience are foreign to their partnered friends, while those with partners, although they may acknowledge that being single might lead to some lonely times, feel that the loneliness they sometimes experience even within their partnership could never be understood by their single acquaintances.

Because of our strong cultural bias we may go so far as to regard aloneness as unhealthy, believing that those who live this way have lost faith and trust in the human race and have shut themselves away to avoid further rejection. It is not unusual for individuals who live alone to be regarded with pity and possibly even in need of therapy.

The tradition that defines psychological health in terms of the time spent with other people is the tradition that has become the societal norm. Aloneness for any length of time is often seen as a symptom of breakdown or maladjustment.

Certainly parents and teachers voice concern over children and young people who choose to be by themselves rather than take part in group activities, and those social isolates who appear to live happily are viewed suspiciously and suspected of hiding deep feelings of rejection and alienation. Being alone is seldom seen as a natural choice made by perfectly healthy individuals who are comfortable with their own company.

The issue of being alone elicits many different responses. At one end of the scale there are those who believe that human beings have a horror of being alone and will go to any lengths to have company. Single people, in this view, are unhappy, unfulfilled individuals, desolate in their aloneness.

At the other end of this scale are those who champion the place of solitude in our lives. In fact, they lament the busy, people-filled lives of most of us, explaining all illness and stress in terms of too much human contact. A good dose of solitude, they insist, is necessary for promoting health, creativity and personal growth.

'In real solitude we are expansive, limitless, free ... We renew contact with ourselves and discover who we are ... we see life as it really is.'[1] So writes Clark Moustakas, who has published extensively on the subject of loneliness and who so obviously values the idea of solitude.

A solitary life

Not very long ago, a friend passed on a piece by May Sarton, a writer who extols the solitary life. 'The Rewards of Living a Solitary Life'[2] was a delightful little article, telling of how a friend of hers had spent what he referred to as 'empty' time — an hour or two in the city with nothing to do — and found that, to his great shock, he thoroughly enjoyed his time alone.

May Sarton asks herself what her friend had feared. 'That, suddenly alone, he would discover that he bored himself, or that there was, quite simply, no self there to meet?'

Now, she says, having experienced the joys of aloneness, he is on the edge of great adventure, about to explore his inner space, and, unencumbered by others, he has a sharper individual perception than ever before. That is because solitude, she tells us, 'is the salt of personhood. It brings out the authentic flavour of every experience'.

I like that. It echoes Paul Theroux's thought, that the word 'alone' is implied in the world's best travel books.[3] The argument is that when we are with others our own experiences become diffused, distracted as we may be by their presence and their thoughts and their responses. To experience alone is to experience most truly, according to both writers. As Sarton says:

> Loneliness is most acutely felt with other people ... Human intercourse often demands that we soften the edge of perception, or withdraw at the very instant of personal truth for fear of hurting, or of being inappropriately present, which is to say naked, in a social situation. Alone we can afford to be wholly whatever we are, and to feel whatever we feel absolutely. That is a great luxury!

These words were particularly enlightening for me at the time of reading. Being alone is not a common personal experience for me, and I am curious about it. Solitary friends tell me about its virtues, and its drawbacks too. One of them has told me:

> Sometimes, after a day with friends, when they all pile into cars to go back home together, I do feel what I would describe as loneliness. It is not something that lasts, and in fact usually by the next morning, when I wake up to birds singing and crisp air and misty skies, I feel fine again. Nature makes a fine and dependable companion for me, and I indulge myself in fantasies, and other colourful imaginings ... the things you have time to do when you are alone ... Being alone can be a liberating situation in the sense that the individual finds the freedom to experience an unusually wide range of emotions, to have either stereotyped or wildly imaginative thoughts, to feel either hellishly miserable or ecstatically happy.[4]

A charming distinction between aloneness and loneliness appears in this excerpt from *The Life of the Mind*:

> ... solitude is that human situation in which I keep myself company. Loneliness comes about when I am alone without being able to split up into the two-in-one, without being able to keep myself company ... or, to put it differently, when I am one and without company.[5]

Considering this model, it is interesting to note that 'being one' in this context refers to that state of disenchantment, that state of fear or shame or anxiety where the self is alienated from itself and so avoids its own company. Splitting into the 'two-in-one', however, refers to that more centred state of being where it is a pleasure to seek out the self for company and know that the time will be enjoyed and even relished.

Another author wrote:

the word 'alone' is a contraction of all and one ... You'll know you have befriended yourself when you enjoy and look forward to periodic time with your all-oneness. In fact, you will feel deprived if you take too little of this time. You'll relish private time with You just as you would with any special friend.[6]

Sounds appealing.

Alone and friendly

To reinforce the idea that aloneness is not the same as loneliness, a number of studies report that quantitative aspects of relationships are not strongly related to feelings of well-being. Quantitative aspects include the number of friends and the frequency of contact with them.

The conclusion is that, where relationships are concerned, the concept of more being better is a simplistic one, and there is a need to turn from questions that reveal quantitative results to questions of how social relationships actually work.

For example, what is it that makes some relationships for some of us so deeply emotionally supportive? And is it preferable to have one intimate friend than to have many acquaintances with whom one doesn't ever quite spill the contents of one's heart?

Some may argue that the answers to these questions depend on the individual; this argument rests on the premise that our feelings very much depend in this case on our own definitions of friendship and intimacy and our expectations with regard to them.

Jenny's story illustrates some aspects of the issue:

I met Sara when I was sixteen years old and new to the local school. We didn't hit it off immediately but gradually became close, as close as sisters, our teachers told us then.

We are both thirty-five years old now, and we've both had partners and children — Tom and I are still together but Sara and Will split five years ago. Despite everything, or maybe even because of everything, we are still very close, and there has never been anyone who means the same to me as Sara does.

Obviously Tom and I are close too, but it's different with a man, even if you are committed to him! I have a number of acquaintances — people I've met through work, or through the children's schooling time — and I like them all very much. We see each other socially, have dinner together, or breakfast, that sort of thing. But finally it's Sara who knows what's in my deepest heart.

Jenny's friend Sara lives with her two teenage children who are more often out than in, and she admits to occasional feelings of loneliness when she is alone.

It isn't overwhelming, though. All I need to remember is how I felt when I was in a marriage that wasn't feeding me in any way — at least now I control my own life and choose to do what I want to do when I want to do it.

Mind you, in the evenings when I'm alone, doing what I want to do usually means reading a book or working on the quilts I'm making for the kids. It's great relaxation after a day at work. Occasionally I get together with Jenny and we catch up on our lives — she is my wonderful confidante and I don't know what I'd do without her. We share everything.

So, I have an intimate friend, a few others I see once in a while, and of course my kids — we're quite close but they are establishing their independence so I see less of them these days. That suits me because I support their growing up and finding themselves without my hovering.

Finally I'd have to say I like my solitude. I actually look forward to going home at the end of the day to a quietish place — I'm probably a bit of a recluse when all's said and done!

It seems that both Jenny's and Sara's needs are well satisfied by each other and by a few others in their lives. Neither has the idea that 'more is better' as far as friendships are concerned, relying more on quality than quantity. Their living arrangements are quite different: where Jenny lives with her partner Tom and three children, Sara is spending more and more time on her own as her children stake out their independence. But time on her own for Sara is something she quite relishes.

Living arrangements, then, cannot predict whether or not an individual will experience loneliness. As one group of researchers noted, 'the absence of others [is] not a negative condition ... solitude [is] clearly not a condition of unmanageable loneliness or misanthrope'.[7]

THE CAPACITY TO BE ALONE
What is it?

In her little book *Loneliness*, Irma Kurtz writes: 'I think true loneliness has very little to do with lack of fellows and almost everything to do with an inability to be alone. Lack of fellows may be an itch, but failure to be content in one's company is a flaming agony.'[8]

The capacity to be alone reflects a measure of security in oneself. It is important not to confuse the pathologically isolated with those who simply enjoy their solitude. The former are individuals who avoid company of any sort and are withdrawn to an unhealthy degree, while the latter have a capacity that allows them a great deal of freedom and enjoyment.

This is not to say that those who have the capacity to be alone necessarily choose much of their time to be on their own. On the contrary, they may thoroughly enjoy others' company, they may feel deeply satisfied with their social network at their place of work and they may lead sometimes busy social lives. But when they are on their own they have no desperate desire to seek out others. They feel comfortable with their own company and look forward to time alone.

Nevertheless, there are many people who do choose to spend much of their time alone and enjoy that extended time on their own too, even though they would not necessarily shun company. These people most certainly have a well-developed capacity to be alone.

It has been suggested that the capacity to be alone in adulthood is based on the infant's experience of being alone in the presence of the mother. Psychoanalyst Donald Winnicott put forward this idea in 'The Capacity to be Alone', a paper he published in 1958 and in which he wrote that 'it is only when alone (that is to say, in the presence of someone) that the infant can discover his personal life'.[9]

Winnicott's theory fits well with Bowlby's theory of attachment in explaining the development of this capacity for aloneness. Remember that Bowlby believed that we form strong bonds — usually with mother — early in life, and that being separated at that stage leads to what he termed separation anxiety.

What he also postulated was that for an infant to develop into a separate person with an individual identity it needs the help of another person, most usually its mother.

Imagine a child being totally secure: with no anxiety about the possibility of the mother, or other attachment figure, disappearing and not returning, and with no anxiety about needing to fulfil others' expectations. This child is able to relax when it is in the presence of the attachment figure — it is able to 'be alone' without yet truly being alone.

As this child grows older, according to this theory, it will be less and less in need of the constant physical presence of the attachment figure — it will have developed the capacity to be alone.

There are a few dimensions at play here: the personality of the child, the state of the mother at that time and the quality of the reassurances, the capacity of the mother herself and the father himself to be alone. Take this story, for instance.

Penny and her husband Mike have often discussed their

quite different responses to being alone. While Penny enjoys it, even relishes it, Mike admits that he busies himself, hoping the time will pass quickly and that someone will arrive home soon. He says:

> I used to think there was something terribly wrong with me. After all, I'm a man, I'm supposed to enjoy independence, time alone and all that. But I realised not so long ago that neither of my parents was comfortable with the idea of time alone — they thought there was something wrong with people who liked to be on their own.
>
> Consequently, they were busy, busy, busy all the time. Socialising, on the phone, on every committee, out talking to neighbours — anything but sit alone and read, or just do nothing. They really wanted us to be busy and involved with other people all the time too.
>
> Penny was encouraged to enjoy her own company, her father died early on, but her mother did this and that on her own and she passed on that ability to be alone to all her kids. I wish I had that capacity.

The capacity to be alone is central to our response when we are in our own company either temporarily or for extended periods. But if it is something we learn early, is it too late for us as adults to learn it? Is there any way we can develop a capacity for aloneness at any time in our life?

The answer, I believe, is an emphatic yes. What it takes is some determination and patience, and we need involve no-one else but ourselves.

Parenting ourselves

We've talked already about the self-concept, and self-esteem. We know that when we feel judged and unworthy we can begin to loathe ourselves, so that to be alone with ourselves is an unbearable thought. When 'the self is out of harmony with itself ... when it is alienated from itself ... it [is] reluctant to be alone with itself'.[10]

We've considered, too, the importance of attachment in infancy and of quality parenting, the sort that allows us to become fully functioning individuals separate from our parents.

Our earliest view of ourselves is based very much on our perceptions of our parents' view of us. The emphasis on perceptions is essential because we need to acknowledge that individuals read input in different ways. Even within families there can be quite wide differences between the ways siblings read the same situation. Being aware of our own individual bias can help us understand how we think about ourselves and how we incorporated the messages all around us when we were small.

Whatever age we are now, we carry with us ourselves at every age we have seen — and, who knows, perhaps more besides. My child is as much of me as is the shy adolescent I was, and the excited young student, and the young woman and the new mother and the older mother.

All of these are part of me, and at some particular times I am acutely aware of one presence amongst them that is interacting strongly with the me of the moment. It is because of this that I can develop the capacity to be alone if I have not already done that.

A friend who has put some time and energy into developing this capacity told me this story:

> I can remember being on my own in a friend's mountain house some time ago and feeling unsure about lasting the weekend alone. There was a pervading sense of danger which I could not pinpoint, and I was tempted at the time to regard it as a foreboding, to pack my bags quickly and to return home. Sheer tiredness kept me there, as well as curiosity tinged with some anxiety.
>
> Relaxing my body, I could sense the fear of a small child telling me to find other people as soon as possible.

'This is not safe here,' she said. 'I need someone to be with me. I am afraid to be alone.'

Turning within to this small child, I talked reassuringly to her — because I was alone, I could speak aloud without fear of being misunderstood! — telling her soothingly that all would be well, all would be well.

'I am with you,' I told her, 'and we are safe. Let's enjoy being away from the crowds just for a short time.' The anxiety diminished, although it never quite disappeared, but subsequent visits alone to the mountain house have been easier and more enjoyable.

Self-parenting is a technique that works in many sorts of situations. Because there are so many parts of us within, we can call on the internalised parent to minister to the frightened, lonely child, just as, in different circumstances, we might call on the fun-loving, carefree child to encourage and enthuse the weary, lonely grown-up in us.

Researchers interested in the antecedents of loneliness have commented that many people, asked what loneliness feels like in their body, report that it is like a hole 'here' — and they point to the chest, or the stomach, or the diaphragm. Having few friends or acquaintances 'might reasonably imply a "hole" in one's social world, but why is this experienced as a hole in the self?'[11]

These researchers report that people have no problem in imagining a solution for their loneliness, and they add that the imagining is often a great surprise to everyone concerned.

Why? Because invariably the solution involves a parent directly or indirectly. They tell of one example of a thirty-year-old woman who, as her solution to loneliness, imagined 'burrowing under' an older male person who was lying down on the ground. She was surprised, when she thought about it, to remember that on Friday evenings her father would come home early, lie down on the floor under a blanket and encourage her to lie snuggled up next to him while they both watched television.

'Most of the "solution images" we have recorded are reminiscent of parent–child relations, although not always in such a concrete way.'[12]

If solutions to loneliness are so very often seen in terms of interaction with, and nurturance and comfort from, our parents, then it makes sense to be our own parents to ourselves when we can. Whatever has gone before, whether or not we have experienced a supportive and loving home environment, we can either continue to nurture ourselves, or begin to know the joys of it.

ALONE — BY CHOICE OR OTHERWISE
Choosing solitude

In *The Call of the Desert — The Solitary Life in the Christian Church*, Peter Anson writes: 'An innate craving for solitude is a not uncommon symptom among mankind in general, in spite of the fact that man is commonly supposed to be a "social animal" ...'[13]

The quest for solitude has a long history: it has emerged amongst all races, in all ages and in all religions.

The Indian Brahman, for example, must pass through four stages, of which that of the 'vanavasin' or anchorite is one. (The term anchorite is derived from the Greek *anakhoretes*, meaning someone of secluded habits.) Buddha — 'the Enlightened' — spent six years in solitude, and later founded communities of men who lived the lives of hermits. And in the Old Testament there are many references to the quest for solitude. The tradition of these Old Testament prophets who lived solitary lives in the wilderness was perpetuated by John the Baptist who in turn inspired many Christian hermits after him.

Each century has seen many solitaries, often affiliated with a religious or spiritual movement; one of the more recent and more renowned was Charles de Foucauld, the French explorer born in the middle of the nineteenth century and on whose teachings a fraternity known as the 'Little Brothers' is based. While the solitaries of early times fled to the wilderness to live in solitude, these solitaries live in the midst of common humanity, in the world of the poor, sharing in their hard life and contributing to the Church through prayer and sacrifice.

The term 'solitude' meant, in ancient times, living outside the bounds of society. The retreat to monasteries or hermitages — the attempt to realise a more ideal community than society at large could ever offer — has been a recurring theme throughout history. This idea of de Foucauld's of the solitary life, which involved leading a hidden life amongst others, was quite a revolutionary one, giving new sense to the meaning of the term 'solitary'.

Within our society most of us are aware of those who choose to live the solitary life. They may be work colleagues who return to their homes alone and who prefer their own company to a more social existence during their non-working hours. They may be regarded as the eccentrics of the neighbourhood, the individuals who shun social contact and keep to themselves most if not all of the time.

While the judgement of them may be that they are running away from the real world, their judgement of others may be that *they* are running away from themselves, immersing themselves in other people so as to avoid facing up to the often harsh realities of the self.

Solo voyagers
There are some individuals who would undertake a solo voyage or stay in their search for renewal. Admiral Byrd, who operated a weather base in the Antarctic alone during 1934, admitted later that, although the overt reason for his vigil was to observe meteorological changes, there was another more significant reason. He had no important purposes, he wrote, none at all, except to discover for himself how good solitude could be.[14]

He described the sense of harmony that he experienced during his time alone, the 'gentle rhythm' as he named it in his diary accounts.

A more recent solo voyager, the Australian Kay Cottee, wrote this entry into her journal about three months after she set off on her historical voyage around the world in 1988:

> Everybody seems so surprised to hear me sounding so cheerful and happy. Guess they can't understand how much I love it out here by myself — no phones, no pressure, just a challenge to live with the elements every day. Peace. I suppose in another three months I'll have had enough of my own company and run out of things to amuse myself with, but for now I wouldn't swap places with anyone in the world ...[15]

Kay Cottee's words would resonate with most of those individuals who choose to live the solitary life: they, too, wouldn't swap places with anyone else in the world, despite what the world may think of their decision.

Enforced solitude

Freely chosen solitude may be regarded as an opportunity for renewal, insight and change, and it may be keenly sought for its benefits and its joys. However, enforced solitude is another matter.

Solitary confinement in prisons has been employed to encourage remorse but it is recognised as a cruel punishment, inducing acute mental instability. For example, it is not unusual for these prisoners to develop obsessional rituals to give some structure to the hours and hours of solitude, and prisoners suffer very intense anxiety if these rituals are interrupted in any way. Self-mutilation and suicide attempts are frequent. If these are the results of solitary confinement in comparatively humane situations, imagine the effects of such confinement in those cases where there is a violation of a whole range of human rights.

The deprivation of sensory input is largely to blame for the mental disruption that results from being confined in a solitary state. With no visual or auditory stimulation over some time, the human spirit can eventually be broken. Research into sensory deprivation began about forty years ago, and revealed that it destroyed coherent thought, increased suggestibility, induced hallucinations and severe panic attacks.

Despite these horrors, there are examples of those who have actually benefited to some extent from enforced partial solitude and alienation from society: the spiritual and mental turmoil they have experienced has found expression later on in their creative works. Dostoevsky, for example, spent time in solitary confinement and was imprisoned later on with no books or writing materials. His prison experience was later described in *The House of the Dead*.

ALONENESS AS A THERAPY

Most of us are familiar with the feeling that we 'must get away from it all'. Removing ourselves from the busyness of everyday life for a time, we return to the fray refreshed to some extent by the break and feeling rather more settled than before.

We live in a bustling society: when human beings are not talking to us and needing our attention, loud music fills the gap, or honking horns, or radio or television or the telephone. Visually we are assaulted every minute that our eyes are open: billboards scream messages, cars flash by, there is constant movement, movement, movement.

We have largely realised our need to remove ourselves from all of this intense stimulation if only for a short time, to recover from the overload and to get in touch with our senses once again. To this extent, solitude is a therapy for us.

The use of solitary therapy goes back a long way; social isolation and a reduction in stimuli have often been used in the treatment of institutionalised patients, and also to help modify bad health habits. We are being bombarded fairly constantly with an overload of sensory input.

'It has taken a long time ... psychologists are beginning to pass the word about the effects of crowding, noise, information overload, future shock, lack of privacy, and the rest. The antidote is solitude, stillness, and time out.'[16] So writes Peter Suedfeld in a paper called 'Aloneness as a Healing Experience'. With fewer frantic distractions, he reminds us, we will be able to learn to acknowledge and appreciate those things that are important in our lives but which we have been driven to ignore.

He points to the fact that when animals are ill or injured they tend to move off into isolation while they are recovering and wonders whether this is a case of evolutionary adaptiveness. If it is, there are implications for humans; perhaps there is a basic need in us to seek out solitude for recovery and improved health physically as well as psychologically and spiritually.

Loneliness may be a threat when we choose to take time out, but the restorative rewards of at least some aloneness in our lives are worth the risk.

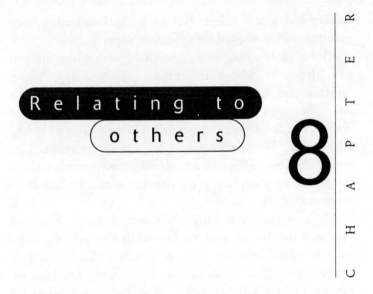

8

RELATIONSHIPS
Why we want them

Relationships satisfy two human requirements: the need for general companionship, for fun with other people and just plain chit-chat about life, and the need for closeness, for sharing important things, and the acceptance and understanding that comes from people close to us.

As we've seen, we practise 'making' relationships from an early age, and during adolescence we have a chance to learn how to refine the process. By the time we reach adulthood most of us have learned how to initiate relationships.

Our motive for initiating them is something else. We've all met the professional socialisers who gather friends the way a headhunter collects heads: it's all in the numbers. What may keep these people going is the fear that, if they stop for long, they will discover a well of loneliness that is too hard to face, let alone fill.

Initiating lots of relationships does not lead automatically to having lots of friends: friendship takes maintenance, and that takes work. Paradoxical as it may seem, maintaining a relationship of any kind requires at least a little solitary work: relationships are two-way processes, involving give and take and some private thought as to one's own needs and those of the other person.

Elena is a young woman who shares a flat with her partner Adam. She has a few very close friends, some from school days and one from work, and a fair circle of acquaintances. On relationships generally she has this to say:

> Some people don't realise how much time you can put into other people — for example, I make sure I phone one or other of my three or four close friends every few days.
>
> I love talking to them, of course, but I also feel a sort of commitment to the relationship. When I call I am really saying 'You are important to me', and when they call me I feel they are saying the same to me. Naturally I set time aside to be with Adam too, which I enjoy, but I can see the importance of doing that quite apart from the enjoyment.
>
> There's no doubt about it — relationships take work, although not in the sense of a burden or a nuisance. It's like anything you love — you take care of it, no matter what it takes to do it.

Being intimate

Whether or not it is a matter of being socially conditioned, most human beings would admit to wanting to be close to at least one other person in the world. However intense our needs for both solitude and privacy, most of us crave the comfort, warmth and understanding that another being can provide for us.

As small children, after the joys of early physical closeness we gravitate towards other small children, sniffing them out like wolf cubs, seeking contact and warmth from those other than our immediate family. Later, the peer group plays a significant role, and we find best friends with whom to share jokes, tell secrets, help each other in difficult situations and set off on daring adventures. With adolescence comes an even greater drive towards the pack despite the push for autonomy and identity. The peer group provides comfort and intimacy at this time. From here through to adulthood we look for 'safe others' — people we can really call friends because of their loyalty and because of mutual trust and understanding.

Some people are lucky enough to have lifelong friendships that are close and fulfilling. Times of intimate sharing may become less frequent between such friends, but the deep bonds remain intact. Others spend much of their lives looking for someone with whom to share their fears and their dreams, but their hearts remain heavy and alone, because no such person seems to make an appearance. For these people life can be frustrating and lonely as they wonder why intimacy escapes them so cruelly.

At what stage do we stop reaching out, as an infant reaches out in total trust and hope, for someone to draw near to us? When do we learn to keep our hands and our arms firmly by our sides, rarely venturing towards another?

Fear of intimacy, most evident in those of us who shy away from being close to others, has a lot to do with the fear of surrendering a part of oneself, or even all of oneself.

Those who have examined intimacy and written thoughtfully, sensitively and provocatively on the subject present the same necessary starting point: knowing oneself, being intimate with that same self. Writer Stephanie Dowrick examines the issue in depth in her book *Intimacy and Solitude*. She writes: 'Intimacy — closeness to yourself in times of solitude or closeness to others in moments of sharing and connecting — reflects your inner world as almost nothing else does. And intimacy begins from the inside; it begins with your own self.'[1]

Here is a launching pad for those searching for intimacy out there in the big, quite frightening world. Beware, though

— the inner world is no less enormous, no less full of dark alleys and unfriendly faces. It is no less confronting and hurtful, but it is manageable, and what's more, it's all ours.

All ours. That in itself is something to savour. Here is an entire forest that belongs entirely to oneself. Like all forests, it can be enchanted. It can be dark and forbidding in places. It can be intriguing, full of burrows and leafy hollows. It can be charming, with lichen and mossy bits creeping over the ancient limbs of massive trees.

It can be alive with great shafts of light that dance and tease. It can be frightening where thorny bushes seem to enclose you in an impenetrable hug. But to work our way to the heart of the forest, bruised, torn and tormented as we may be, is to work towards the centre of our own soul and to know ourselves more than we could ever have imagined.

To be close to someone, to be intimate with them, means to hear them and to understand them. Is it possible to offer that to someone else but not be able to offer it to ourselves? I think not. It is difficult, if not impossible, to give effectively to others what we deny to ourselves.

If we believe we are giving out but denying ourselves, then we need to examine our motives. Carers, whether they be mothers, counsellors or friends, who ignore their own needs and put their all into filling the needs of their child, client or friend, are not partaking of an intimate relationship. Intimacy requires give and take, a balance of vulnerability and strength, empathy and total trust.

Possession is sometimes mistaken for intimacy. Unpalatable as this may sound, it is a convenient choice for those who are afraid to be alone, and who are afraid to look inwards too closely.

A 'merger' relationship — where a couple seems to be deeply mutually caring and there is little time for anyone or anything else, is another pitfall. Certainly on the surface this kind of relationship can appear to be an intimate one, but there is a loss of identity on the part of both involved. Their closeness, which others may envy, is actually an unhealthy merging of two characters so that neither knows where they begin and where they end.

What feeds intimacy is authenticity, together with the willingness to share ourselves. However, while we have a need to reveal ourselves, we also have a need to conceal ourselves.

Conceal ourselves we do well. Some use silence to keep others at bay. Others chatter incessantly, rarely drawing breath to let others break in, while others again discuss theories, or make academic observations. Our shields are many and effective. Securely placed behind them, we wail 'I want to be close to someone', as we eye those other shields all about us.

Becoming attached

We have seen how loneliness emulates the experience of separation anxiety which has been a subject of great interest to many, among them John Bowlby who has written extensively on the subject of 'attachment behaviour', the distinctive feature of which he believed was attaining or maintaining proximity to another.

Infants, Bowlby noted, engage in this behaviour, and parents complement it by engaging in caregiving behaviour. This pair of behaviours together results in what he referred to as 'affectional bonding', the deep and strong bonding between two individuals which first occurs during infancy. What's more, he wrote: '... the patterns on which a person's affectional bonds are modeled during adult life are determined to a significant degree by events within his family of origin during childhood ...'[2]

Bowlby saw affectional bonding as part of our biological inheritance, which helps to explain his scientific approach to the subject. He talked of human beings engaging firstly in attachment and then later in 'pair formation' — getting together with a special other person and becoming mutually attached.

So it is that the process of drawing close to another echoes an earlier process: but whereas in the first case the relationship is uneven in that the caregiver gives all for the well-being of the infant, in the case of adults who become attached to each other each learns to anticipate and satisfy the needs of the other.

Not all caregivers are so nurturing, however. Some who have not been nurtured themselves repeat the family pattern of neglect; some who have been abandoned have no idea how to nurture; some who yearn to be nurtured have no resources for any other. And some who believed that an infant would fill their pit of loneliness discover early that it is an impossible task to ask of anyone else, let alone a dependent baby. Their response is despair.

The reasons for faulty bonding are many: whatever they are, the modelling is inadequate and there are many individuals who spend time wondering at their loneliness, at their sense of alienation and isolation, at their unsuccessful attempts to establish strong and effective ties with others, without recognising that the cause lies deep in their psyches.

Sometimes it takes becoming a parent to confront these issues. Perhaps that is because parenting a child harks back to an earlier time and we project our own inner child onto this new physical baby. We may remember, sometimes in painful detail, the inadequacies of the parenting offered to us, and we come to understand better the reasons for our sense of loneliness: if that initial bonding was not achieved satisfactorily a baby can be left feeling confused, frightened and isolated. Who else is there to turn to but a parent or caregiver after all?

If that initial affectional bonding is established in a healthy way — if parents can offer all to their tiny child just for the sake of its well-being and not out of an attempt to satisfy their own hungry soul — then that child is likely to begin developing a healthy self-image. The separation anxiety that all babies experience to some degree would tend to be quelled more easily in this child, and to be alone would be seen less as an abandonment and more of a welcome time for solitary pleasures.

As an adult, attachment to others involves an easier, clearer process when early role modelling has been effective, when we have witnessed our elders engaging in mutually satisfying relationships that are open and loving and allow space for growing. These are relationships that allow for our full humanity to be expressed, together with the support and nurturance that is required along the way.

It isn't just our parents who provide our role-models though: more and more our society has relied on a whole range of input to educate our young, and certain cultural norms, however damaging they may be to the growth and awareness of the individual, have become the stuff of magazines, books, movies and television. One of these is the notion of romantic attachment.

Falling in love

Here is a most potent experience, involving intense feelings fired by desire and longing. Driven by such an idea, we seek out the one with whom to share such a wildly delicious encounter.

Herein lies the idea of romantic attachment. But we must beware, as Robert Johnson, eminent Jungian psychologist, warns us, because this attachment does not mean loving someone but, rather, that we are 'in love', in which state we truly believe that the meaning of life has been magically revealed in this other human being. 'We feel we are finally completed, that we have found the missing part of ourselves ... the package includes an unconscious demand that our lover or spouse always provide us with this feeling of ecstasy and intensity.'[3]

But how can this be possible? While we are attached to our assumptions and expectations, however deeply buried in our subconscious they may be, we will continue to be disappointed and feel tricked. Those like Johnson who tell us that romantic love is merely a traditional Western myth that keeps us looking — looking for the perfect partner who will make us whole — also warn us that although we look around and see that this approach is not working, we persist with it.

As Johnson points out, despite the ecstasy we feel when we are 'in love', we still experience great loneliness, alienation and frustration because our relationships don't seem to be genuinely loving, or committed. 'Usually we blame other people for failing us; it doesn't occur to us that perhaps it is we who need to change our own unconscious attitudes — the expectations and demands we impose on our relationships and on other people.'[4]

Like all relationships, one between romantic partners needs work, and more work than most because of the level of intimacy required to keep it healthy and successful. Rosie is a young woman in her late twenties who has been living with Rick for five years. Here's what she has to say:

> For the first few months, I was so 'in love' with Rick that all I saw was this projection of what I thought was perfect in a man. He was loving, gentle, tender, attentive ... what more could I want?
>
> But suddenly — Pow! — he was just human, and I felt tricked. Here he was doing ordinary things — and here was I doing ordinary things, and the whole thing collapsed. We decided, after a temporary split, to try again with more realistic ideas. It's been really hard sometimes, but we both think it's worth putting effort into a relationship that is basically working for us both.

For Rosie and her partner their relationship was worth a commitment because, once the initial urgency of sexual attraction had waned and the early novelty had turned into familiarity, they found they cared deeply for each other and were prepared to knuckle down to the hard work of relating on a day-to-day basis for the long term. What might have happened, and commonly does happen, was that the two lovers would have begun to recognise aspects of the other's caregiving behaviour that did not suit them. They might have felt bored, or disappointed, or lonely in the company of the other and begun to yearn for a relationship that was more deeply satisfying.

Research indicates that various aspects of a marital relationship are adversely affected by attachment styles that show early distress.[5] Communication between the couple, their problem-solving abilities, their sexual relations and the level and extent of their confiding and care for each other are often unsatisfactory. Both partners report feeling alone and lonely, usually without realising that it is their early experiences that lie behind their current behaviour.

Maintaining relationships

The maintaining of relationships, especially intimate ones, can be extremely difficult, as Rosie says, if not downright impossible. To maintain a relationship we need to be asking ourselves quite regularly how things are going — not just a superficial check, but a real focus on whether our needs and those of our partner are being met in the relationship. It takes, too, an awareness of just how our early history has influenced the way we relate to our partner.

We also need to accept our own individuality and that of our partner, as well as the fact that while we regard ourselves as a couple, we are quite separate individuals. This is an important aspect, because often couples merge into each other, taking on each other's beliefs, attitudes and interests at the expense of their own, in the belief that this is what being a couple means. The consequence can be a deeply felt loneliness that can come as quite a shock — and we might ask, how can I be lonely when I am enmeshed with another human being?

The reply is: very easily, because our self has lost its voice and, what's more, has become squashed and overlooked because the 'couple self' has taken over. Ironically, this sort of merging comes out of the fear of aloneness, but ultimately it is because of the merging that great loneliness is felt. M. Scott Peck, in his book *The Road Less Travelled*, tells us that when we love in a genuine way we respect the individuality of our loved one, and we do what we can to cultivate it, even if it may mean separation or even loss. In words that echo Jung's, he writes that our ultimate goal in life is to grow spiritually, to experience the journey we take on our own 'to peaks that can be climbed only alone ... It is the return of the individual to the nurturing marriage or society from the peaks he or she has traveled alone which serves to elevate that marriage or that society to new heights.'[6]

This is one of my favourite pieces from that book, especially the idea of 'the solitary journey to peaks that can be climbed only alone' and the elevation of the marriage or society when the lone traveller returns. The rewards of genuine love are great, but then so are the risks. Few of us dare to encourage fully the individuality of a partner — even the notion of it can stir up surges of separation anxiety.

If we decide to perpetuate the myth of romantic attachment, how can we encourage our partner's individuality when that person is part of us, the part we may have once thought was missing? If our partner is busy pursuing other personal interests, where are we in the scheme of things, and how can we survive alone?

Sure enough, the myth of romantic attachment has been responsible for more unhappy relationships than much else: for individuals who feel that, at last, they have bonded with a significant other person in their lives who will be there for them forever and who will continue to make life exciting and meaningful, the myth becomes a cruel joke.

Ironically, love can actually intensify our sense of separation from others because the nature of it leads us to long for there to be no space between us. But 'if love is undertaken as a distraction from loneliness or a "cure" for the very separateness it ought to celebrate, then love must disappoint, and the affair is only a nod between strangers.'[7]

Many a lonely person has been initiated into the process of being 'in love' and been bitterly disappointed. But the process can be a tremendous learning ground: it can help reveal to us the nature of attachment for us, what we look for to satisfy our deepest longings, and our expectations of others — especially significant others — in our lives.

Love and attachment style

What emerges quite clearly in the process of falling in love is our attachment style, the way of relating to others that we learnt from our early experiences with our primary caregiver. In Chapter Four we distinguished between these styles: secure attachment, anxious/ambivalent attachment, and avoidant attachment, each of which is a direct result of our early interactions.

Studies have explored the link between our attachment style and our adult love style and found significant similarities.[8]

Those of us who experienced responsive and caring parenting tend to enjoy more secure and satisfying relationships as adults. We may feel lonely sometimes, but it is a temporary state only.

Those of us who were 'partially reinforced' — sometimes receiving attention and care and at other times either being ignored and neglected, or else having a parent who was intrusive and therefore not sensitive to our needs — will tend to cling in relationships and to be fearful and tense. We tend to try hard for others' acceptance of us, using self-disclosure to draw people close or else other anxious pursuing tactics. We probably often feel lonely, but we don't feel despairingly lonely.

Those of us who experienced early rejection become steadily more and more distant from others — from peers and from family — and as adults we oscillate between regret about this distance and feeling defiant about going our own way. It is possible to change this style by recognising and accepting the painful experiences that have led to our current style and being open to help from others — perhaps through therapy — which helps us come to terms with painful memories.

Living happily ever after

I never questioned, when I was very small, whether my favourite fairytale people would really 'live happily ever after'. When the story was ended, I remember a dreamy feeling wafting over me as I imagined them walking into forever, arms linked, hearts entwined, rather Disney-like. Ahhh, the magic of it all.

When I was a little older I started to wonder why the story ended there. Why didn't it cover at least the first few years of togetherness?

When I was much older and much more cynical I decided I knew why. Where was the magic in the nitty gritty, in the inevitable boredom of everyday life together? What if the Prince became more than a little annoyed at Sleeping Beauty's habit of nodding off whenever he didn't provide some action? And what if Cinderella took her non-assertiveness into her relationship — would her Prince tire of her tendency to play victim?

It's a cruel blow to discover that 'happily ever after' is a myth. Most of us move into a committed relationship with high hopes and trust that we will find more happiness here than anywhere else in the world. But before long the rot sets in — little resentments here, big hurts there, misunderstanding, conditional acceptance, anger, recriminations.

Little by little the relationship is corroded to such an extent that its original purpose and meaning is irretrievably lost and inevitably partners look to each other to cast blame.

Does it have to be this way? Is having a wonderfully fulfilling and loving relationship while growing as an individual just a pipe dream?

Behind the 'happily ever after' syndrome is a hidden agenda. For example, you will like the things I like and the people I like, you will fulfil my unmet needs, you will always know how I feel, you will make me feel complete as a person. It isn't long before each partner realises that their own hidden agenda is not being followed. The choice then is either to protect, or to want to learn more, both about ourselves and our partner. Unfortunately, for most of us most of the time, the choice has been to protect.

Protecting is motivated by a fear of experiencing the emotional pain that may be generated by any conflict. To protect ourselves we might comply, going along with our partner so that we aren't rejected, or we might try to control our partner, or we may shut off, showing indifference and withdrawing altogether.

Whichever of these three paths of protection we choose, we are avoiding taking responsibility for our own feelings and behaviour. The paradox of protection is that, rather than leading to the happiness we think will ensue from avoiding feeling bad, what follows is boredom, deadness, no fun, no joy, and ultimately feelings of intense loneliness.

These protections may be operating very subtly, with each partner manipulating the other like a puppet with invisible strings. One partner, with a deep need for approval, will run ragged trying to please, only to be met with the silent treatment, which is merely non-verbal disapproval. A protective circle of compliance and control is in progress.

Or, because I fear losing myself if I surrender myself to you in any way, I make sure that I rarely fall in with your wishes while you, in turn, do the same. In trying not to lose ourselves, we each lose touch with our natural selves and therefore, of course, with each other.

Because our protections can be so very subtle, we find it difficult to recognise them, let alone acknowledge them. We often like to think that we are open and loving, but brutal self-honesty is essential if we really want to enjoy a truly fulfilling relationship.

We need to ask: What is motivating me here? Am I really feeling loving, or am I feeling dependent/needy/unsure/lonely? Is my 'openness' a ploy to make the other open up too, or do whatever else I want? What are my underlying fears at this moment? The first step to greater self-understanding and deeper intimacy with another is to become aware of these underlying fears and to move while still feeling afraid.

That takes a lot of courage.

We learned very early how to prevent ourselves from experiencing emotional pain and we tend to automatically react that way now. Staying open is an enormous challenge and one met by relatively few people.

'There is a true delight in the realisation that someone knows what is going on inside you — that someone knows the *real person* you are,'[9] write David Jansen and Margaret Newman, authors of *Really Relating*. When each of you knows the other, they add, it is because of the hard work you have put into the relationship, and because of your great courage and your maturity. Now comes the reward for your devotion to a special task: the search for the deepest self of your partner. 'Other people see our outward shell — we experience our true selves from the inside. Intimacy and love are ways of both being and expressing the *real self*.'[10]

In the ideal relationship, where both partners have the freedom to grow as individuals with the support and love of each other, exploring together becomes an exciting voyage of discovery. It is when we open to each other that the story really begins.

Sharing who we are

Broadly speaking, to communicate with another person is to share our experience. It may involve verbal or non-verbal contact, and it involves two basic forms of information: the cognitive type, which refers to facts about the world and about ourselves, and the affective type, which refers to feelings and emotions.

Factual information is most usually communicated verbally, but our feelings and emotions are more usually communicated non-verbally because our conscious mind is less able to censor this style of communication.

Often, then, we know more about a person because of what they didn't say (but expressed facially and bodily anyway) than because of what they've told us. Similarly, we often reveal more about ourselves non-verbally than we do verbally.

For those of us lucky enough to have an empathic listener, a person who listens beyond the spoken words and responds to our feeling level of expression, there can be the experience of genuine communication. For the rest, trying to communicate can be a frustrating and lonely experience.

This works in various ways. If, for example, I am trying to tell you about something important to me and you can't hear what I am saying, I might feel alienated and alone. If I would like to tell you something but can't find the words, and you are not interested enough to help me find them, then again, I might feel very alone.

And if you are wanting to know more about me but I am full of mistrust and have built a wall around my soul, then you might feel shut out by me and consequently alone and lonely. My wall keeps me isolated from others and myself too, so that we two may live together under the same roof but we both feel alone and isolated.

Communication is central to the building and maintaining of relationships: we tell each other who we are through communication of one sort or another, and we pretend to tell each other who we are too. We also try to tell each other who we are not — perhaps because we aren't sure ourselves of who we truly are, or because we reject who we are in favour of an image that seems more attractive and acceptable.

It is through communication that we tell another person that we value them and that they are important to us; and it is through communication that we tell another person that they mean nothing to us. We may use verbal communication or we may transmit our messages non-verbally. In the end, how we feel comes across loud and clear.

All that we do has a message for anyone who is looking, and for those of us who feel distrustful, or anxious about separation, or disdainful, or hopeless, our message is a warning to others: Keep away! Take care here! Don't get caught! Our words may seem inviting but our real message tells another story.

Communication between people has also been referred to as 'dialogue', '... the essential element of every social interaction ... the elixir of life.'[11] James Lynch, author of *The Broken Heart*, describes dialogue as 'reciprocal, spontaneous, often nonverbal and *alive*',[12] and tells us that the very guidelines for communication that our society tries to sell us, guidelines as to how we can make friends, how we should behave towards our lover, how we should speak to the people in our lives, often seem to cause a disruption in dialogue, keeping us isolated and lonely.

There is no learning of rules for genuinely communicating with those who are significant in our lives, or initiating relationships we might enjoy. We may learn some techniques — for example, how to start a conversation, where to look, what to say next, how often to nod knowingly and to murmur words of understanding.

In the workshops on communication that I have run or helped to run, people are always keen to discuss ways to improve how they talk with others, and how they listen. They recognise the importance of communicating in helping our lives to run smoothly, and also in keeping our relationships healthy and vital. But while certain strategies may prove useful, true communication can come only from expressing who we are in essence. There is no way around it: getting to know and understand ourselves as thoroughly as we can and being prepared to continue in our self-learning is the best start to being able to share communication satisfyingly with others.

THE OTHER SIDE OF RELATING
Unhealthy 'love'

Relationships certainly take work, but we must be careful to distinguish between healthy effort — the requirement for a reciprocal relationship in which we can grow — and unhealthy effort. Robin Norwood, discussing *Women Who Love Too Much* says that the women of whom she writes spend much of their time and energy, in fact much of their lives, trying to change a person who is unable to love them into someone who can. Although it never works, it provides some safety because the long and fruitless struggle keeps them from having to face up to being truly intimate and letting anyone else ever know them very deeply. 'Most people are so frightened of that. So while their loneliness drives them toward relationships, their fear causes them to choose people with whom it won't ever really work.'[13]

Here is a most important distinction and we can make it for ourselves by examining our own pattern of relating. Do we try too hard? Are we hell-bent on filling the well of emptiness that sits inside us? Are we desperate not to let someone go, even when all the signs are telling us that the time has come?

The answers are not always obvious, and may require some thorough soul-searching, best undertaken on our own. Solitude can be a helpful friend to us in sorting chaff from grain.

After the end

Maintenance of a relationship requires a good deal of effort, and while we may be prepared to put that level of energy into something we consider worthwhile, there are times when relationships do wind up.

When people talk of loneliness, they most often talk about the rupturing or discontinuation of a relationship as the prime cause. One young woman says: 'I feel loneliest after ending any sort of a relationship, whether it's long-term or short-term; feeling lonely for me is like feeling lost and having nowhere to focus.'

For some, feeling lost and having nowhere to focus means just one thing: find another relationship fast! But for others it is an opportunity. As the same young woman says, in commenting on what she has done about the way she felt when she has been lonely: 'I have found something to focus upon, to absorb my mind and also to make me want to focus on myself and appreciate myself.'

When we are younger, most of us look forward to the time when we find a steady partner; whether we think that far ahead or not, we probably imagine that we will be together on a long-term basis, essentially sharing life together.

As Rosie found, though, reality has a habit of butting in, and even if we do find someone to settle down with, it isn't long before we have to face it. That's when some of the crises of life really make themselves felt, with partners feeling misunderstood, cheated, disappointed, discouraged, even devastated.

And it's when loneliness can also make itself felt, when a person can ultimately turn to no-one else but only inwardly to understand themselves and to hear what steps they need to take. As one young man put it:

> Some people I know are so afraid of loneliness they run from relationship to relationship without having fully resolved either their own personal feelings and 'who they are', or the residual hurt, rejection, sadness and pain from previous relationships. Fear of loneliness is a real motivating factor in these cases.

Pressure to partner

The strong 'couple-mentality' of our society is the force behind feelings of loneliness for many people: despite the fact that so many choose to live alone, there is still the message that to be partnerless is to be an oddity.

To be part of a couple tends to be a valued social role and so has considerable status attached to it: our success is measured not only by what we own — our material wealth — but also by what relationships we have achieved.

Paul is a young man who feels the pressure of having no permanent partner.

People joke about my bachelor status, especially the fellows at work who are all in long-term relationships. I am twenty-eight now, and I've only ever had a couple of girlfriends, but now I feel ready for something permanent.

I feel really lonely sometimes when there's a whole group of us out, and the others all have their partners, especially when they rib me about how I'm alone. Somehow I think people would even respect me more if I had a partner.

Not everyone feels as Paul does about being part of a couple.

Gabrielle, who is twenty-nine, says:

It used to be just my parents who hinted about my settling down with just one person rather than having various people to go out and enjoy life with. They would tell me about their friends' kids getting married — 'It's about time, too', they'd say about someone younger than I was! It bugged me, their attitude was all so old-fashioned and out of date, but I tried not to let it worry me.

But then friends started settling down in pairs two or three years ago, and they began saying things like 'Come on Gabbi, jump in! It's great! Do it now! You'll end up lonely if you don't!' A few of them tried setting up blind dates for me, but I flatly refused to be involved and although they laughed it off, I could tell they were irritated with me and thought I was just being stubborn and proud.

The fact is that they would feel more comfortable having me around if I was half of two. It's easier having a couple around than a single. Sometimes I really think some people feel threatened that I am on my own.

It is that old horror of aloneness that is often at play here; if we have a fear of being alone then the way of life of an individual who is living alone can be both confronting and threatening to us. It may challenge our own entrenched 'couple mentality', but it could also remind us of an option we turned away from, and perhaps for the wrong reasons.

The challenge of partnering

How many individuals couple in order to escape the possibility of loneliness? How many cling to the idea of finding 'the right person' — a euphemism for 'the one who will fulfil my needs always and who will protect me from loneliness'?

Here is a real trap with a painful snare: if this is the motivation for coupling, the reality proves fatal to the individual. Not only can no other person fill our every need and protect us from feelings of loneliness, but we will be feeling more alone than ever if we try merging ourselves with another.

The challenge for those who couple is to maintain their individual sense of self while sharing their lives with others. There is no doubt about it: it takes sheer hard work and determination. In this couple-centred culture the energy required to sustain a healthy relationship side by side with a healthy self is underestimated and, I believe, barely acknowledged.

The myth of 'happily ever after' is firmly entrenched and its promise — of a carefree life now that the hard work of the chase and the catch are over — more damaging than storytellers could imagine.

It takes mature human beings to recognise that partnership, while providing companionship, is demanding and tough at times. Time for solitude and contemplation is often more limited and, if we agree that the world is a mirror for us, those of us in a partnership are confronted with a relentless mirror day after day.

All this is not to undermine the value of partnership or of relationships generally. But for those of us who have bought into the cultural prescription that to be 'half of a couple' is what makes our lives worthwhile, it gives pause for thought.

When we enter a relationship, any relationship, with a healthy sense of self and an interest in further growth both for ourselves and for the other, then we are seeing relationship at its best: an opportunity to evolve as a human being with the support of another person.

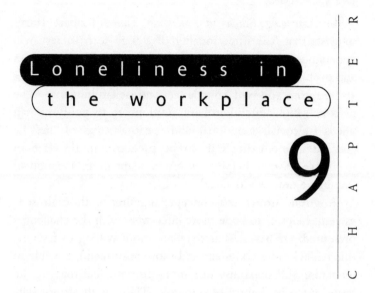

CHAPTER 9

AT WORK
Facing change

Few of us have been unaffected by the vast changes involved in moving from an industrial society to a technology and information society. For some of us the changes may have been comparatively minor so far but for many others the changes have brought upheaval together with feelings of insecurity and fear. In his classic work on the subject, Alvin Toffler defined what he called 'future shock', a condition of very great anxiety especially for those unable to cope with the change involved in such a vast transition.

Because of the changes in the structure of work as we have known it, and its processes, certain jobs are continuing to become obsolete and for those who retain their positions at least some retraining is usually required. The consequence is that many of us are made vulnerable to a significant amount of stress because of the rapid rate of change which can leave us feeling powerless, apathetic and alienated.

In *Managing People in Changing Times*, Robert Burns suggests that 'the impersonality of a high-tech society will generate the demand for more satisfying personal relationships and groups',[1] as well as movements whose central principle is an emphasis on self-knowledge and self-fulfilment. 'The personal, high-touch corollary develops ... to satisfy human needs in social, emotional and spiritual areas of life,' he continues, and exhorts us to be proactive in the face of inevitable change, helping others to adapt in anticipation of 'the brave new world ahead'.

A good, strong self-concept, together with high self-esteem, helps us to cope more effectively with the challenges presented: we have less anxiety, are more willing to try new things, feel more confident and more resourceful, are able to recognise and maximise our strengths, and feel that we are fairly much in control of our lives. Those with a poor self-concept and poor self-esteem, however, are generally unable to cope with the new challenges and feel that they have no control over what happens to them. In times of such enormous and rapid change they are likely to feel isolated and alienated in what they perceive as an isolating and alien world.

While we most usually think of loneliness in the context of evenings alone, of relationship problems, and of other personal crises, loneliness is a common problem in the workplace. If we lack a sense of purpose in the work that we do, either because our work environment has become foreign to us as a result of extensive changes or for other reasons, then we can feel like strangers in a strange land, carrying out tasks that require no more than automatic responses.

Finding meaning in work

Most of us need to feel that we contribute something of value in our work, even when the financial reward is the main reason for working at a particular job. Regaining our power means that our self-worth is fed: we see ourselves as worth-while human beings who can achieve goals co-operatively.

For some of us, the goal of the company or business for which we work is a worthwhile goal in itself, even when the major goal is to outdo competitors and come out on top in terms of market share.

'It's just a game,' one businessman told me. 'People get so upset at the idea of making money, somehow it's seen as dirty work, but I see it as a game. People who are in the game know the rules, so they are less likely to get hurt than other people think. I've got everything I need, and I don't need more money as such, but I love the thrill of the chase.'

This man is lucky to enjoy what he does, but not everyone feels the same way. When we are employees of a company that pushes towards greater profits we can very easily feel that our work is meaningless, especially if we don't even share in the final rewards.

One woman who works in an office talked of 'putting my office persona on in the morning — my face, my clothes, my shoes, my hair — and spending all day doing something meaningless while the real me is waiting to go home and let it all hang out'.

It is not surprising, then, that many of us feel alienated in the workplace. Caught up in meaningless tasks, lost in a swirl of technological change and wearing work-time masks, we can quickly lose touch with who we are and what our own individual goals and purpose in life might be. The company, after all, is not there to serve us, and it is up to us to align ourselves with its goals: we may be rewarded for lifting profits or sales or doing more for the company, but what we do in that context represents only a part of who we are.

We are fortunate indeed if, in our daily work, we can find outlets for our creativity and initiative. Certainly for those who are self-employed or who work on their own the advantages are that natural talents and interests can be employed, and, as well, there is at least some degree of control over work surroundings and time scheduling. There are disadvantages, too, however.

Steven, a freelance writer, says:

There are a lot of people I meet who are envious of the sort of work I do. They tend to think it is glamorous and that I have hours of free time to do what I would like. The good things about my work are that I can be based in my own study at home and I choose my own hours of work.

The disadvantages are that I have to be very self-disciplined to complete work on time. That means staying up all night sometimes to meet deadlines, when other people are out playing or warm in bed. Another thing is that, caught up in these deadlines, you can become very isolated from other people. I have to watch that, because I have been accused of being married to my job and shutting people out. It isn't that I consciously choose to do that, but it is a side-effect of the work.

Generally this sort of work suits me very well — I know its pitfalls and I try to avoid them, but I don't think the reality of the job would suit many people out there. I happen to believe that most people like to walk away at five in the afternoon and not give work a second thought.

Steven may be right, but perhaps people would bother to give work a second thought if it was meaningful to them in the first place. The counter-argument is that it is our own responsibility to find meaning in our work. This may sound trite, but I have seen it in action. At my local supermarket, for example, I was often impressed by a young woman who made it a real pleasure to have my trolley-full checked out.

She was cheerful and warm, taking care with each item while being quick and efficient, engaging in appropriate chit-chat, and obviously enjoying what she was doing. Most customers gave her positive feedback in the form of warmth and gratitude. A job that for most of us would be tedious and meaningless had been taken on by this young woman in a most impressive way.

This is not to say that it is always possible to inject a job with meaning and enthusiasm. Many of us have held jobs that no amount of enthusiasm would have transformed, and the best course of action is often to move on.

With little or no meaning in what we do, it is easy to feel alienated in our workplace because we have no relationship with our work and are unlikely, then, to foster a relationship with other people.

There can be exceptions: one young man, a tertiary student, earns money for books and entertainment by answering phones for a bulk-order warehouse.

> It is the most boring job you could imagine, and some of the people I talk to are impossible. I could never work there on my own because, apart from being bored, not being able to have an occasional laugh with other people would leave me feeling terribly isolated.
>
> But there are some other people about my age who work when I do, and we agree on how awful it is, and how we do it only for the money which is not bad at all. It's this camaraderie among us that keeps me going sometimes, and they've said the same thing.

Relationships at work

At work we can enjoy some degree of interaction with others even if we would not choose them as close friends. All the same, a large proportion of partnerships begin in the workplace as do all sorts of other relationships.

One friend of mine still meets regularly with a group she began working with twenty-five years ago. Because it is only every few months that they meet, there is always plenty to catch up on, and while they have not shared intimate relationships, each is interested in the others' lives, their difficulties and their strategies for overcoming them. Another friend meets at breakfast in the city with a group of former co-workers for all birthdays and other special occasions. This has become, over the years, a ritual that keeps old friendships alive and intact.

While many people make friends at work, there are others who find this a difficult process and feel marginalised because of the difficulty. We need to remind ourselves that work, while a large part of our lives, is not all our lives, and for some of us it may be more appropriate to build on relationships outside the workplace. If all we have in common with colleagues is the work we do then perhaps we should leave the interactions to that arena.

Because of the work-mask that we may have to keep by our door to put on as we leave in the morning, other people at work may only once in a while have a glimpse of who we are. Work is generally not a place where we can reveal intimate details of our lives. Consequently, those who require a higher level of intimacy in friendship may find work a frustrating experience, not being able to show who they really are, and not being shown by others working around them who they are either.

Trapped in a hierarchy

The organisation of a hierarchy probably was established way back in ancient Mesopotamia. Over the millennia since, structures have evolved this way and that, but today the main form is the hierarchical structure of business companies. The very nature of any hierarchy is to keep those at the top and those at the bottom quite distinct and separate.

It has been suggested[2] that the vertical separation in such a hierarchy, because of the enhancing bias of those at the top and the diminishing bias of those lower down, implies that those at or near the top are better than others.

This differentiation causes obvious problems: we may be working only for the money we need, or we may have in mind to work our way up the ladder, but either way feeling diminished in relation to others in the workplace is not conducive either to productivity or to personal satisfaction.

The further down the ladder the less say we have in the organisation's goals or in any process of change that those up top may decide on. On this subject, Carla tells her story:

> The 'power from above' syndrome was well illustrated to me in my first real job after graduating. I was employed by a large multi-national company in the market research department which was made up in those days of only about twenty-five people. It was interesting work for a while, but then the budget was cut to our department so that there was much less to do. Our salaries continued, and staff were not retrenched, but there was simply too little money to carry out much research of importance.
>
> With the maturity of experience, I might have taken a different course, but at the time as a young person eager to do important things in the world, it was a frustrating experience and I left the company feeling that, because of a decision made by the executives of the company, my hands had been tied and I had no alternative but to leave.

That was at a time when work may have been easier to find, but these days the feelings of helplessness that come from unilateral decision-making cannot always be dealt with so easily. We may need to keep on at a job regardless, and unless we come up with coping strategies we are likely to experience the sense of alienation common to many who find themselves in this situation.

While feelings of helplessness are understandable under some circumstances, it is important to keep in mind that 'being employed, whether changes are going on or not, entails forfeiture of some control over self and the environment'.[3] Having accepted that fact, we can turn our attention to finding solutions to any difficulties at work; casting blame on our employer and our work conditions gives us an excuse for feeling out of control and keeps us from a more proactive approach: casting about with enthusiasm for other options.

Managers and executives need to recognise the importance of employee participation: when employees feel that they have some degree of control over, and some say in, the processes of change they are likely to be more highly motivated, more personally satisfied, and therefore more productive.

The role of work

Work provides a social identity, and this is painfully evident among those who are retrenched. The blow goes beyond loss of pay. Retrenchment represents a stripping of identity which can cause extreme psychological damage. Even retirement can cause distress, especially for those whose entire identity has been bound to their employment.

An elderly man talked to me of this overwhelming sense of emptiness and uselessness since he had stepped down as chairman of the firm. 'Nothing prepared me for this,' he said sadly. 'I have a family and I want for nothing materially, but I feel I don't fit in anywhere now. Once, when I got up in the morning, I knew who I was — the chairman and a busy, successful accountant. Now, I'm not sure.'

Studies reveal that, in answer to the question 'Who am I?', the individual's occupation is invariably mentioned. This indicates the extent to which identity is bound up with work. My occupation reveals a lot more than whether I am employed in some way — it also hints at whether I tend to be conservative or radical, ambitious or not, where I live and with whom, and perhaps more besides.

If I don't 'work' then I have no answer. We are seeing very slow changes in attitudes towards work, but the work ethic is still strong. We value certain kinds of work to the extent that an individual's sense of worth is threatened by lack of it. To work or not to work becomes more of a moral issue than an economic one because of the value attached to being employed.

'Work, work, what would we do without you? Plugging up the holes in my life with work as if it were wood and I a sinking ship.'[4] So wrote Kate Llewellyn. We can use work to avoid making decisions or facing loneliness. When we avoid, however, what needs to be confronted seems to creep up behind us and push us into awareness, if we are lucky. If we are not so lucky it just lurks there, casting its great shadow so that we can't live in the light, but we can't manage to shift the darkness, and while we feel its presence most dreadfully, we are never pushed into action by it.

A family man told me:

> I became aware that I was staying back at work when there was a lot going on at home. Three little kids mean an awful lot of noise and activity, and I stayed away using work as an excuse. I would feel, when I went home, that my wife was too exhausted to talk with me and I felt lonely and shut out of our family life, even though the chaos drove me mad.
>
> Then one of the kids became ill, and later on, with all the stress of that, so did my wife. It turned out to be an opportunity for us to reassess our lives. I'm home much earlier these days, and much more involved. Having them both so ill made me realise how much I value them all and I had to confront my habit of running away from involvement with them by creating more and more work.

For many people Monday morning can't come too soon after Friday afternoon. The weekend is more of a nuisance, a very lonely time that drags on interminably. Saturday and Sunday are often cited as the loneliest days of the week, no doubt because it is then that we are most acutely aware that those around us are involved in social activities with friends or in family outings and experiences.

Work may sometimes be a healthy escape from demands and expectations. One woman says:

> If I didn't go out to work every day, I know my elderly parents would be on the phone or the doorstep as often

as they could manage. I love them, and I do what I can for them, but it seems to be never enough.

The only language they understand is 'I am too busy', so I keep myself just that way. I keep myself safe from invasion by going to work.

Assuming that this woman enjoys her work, perhaps it is less of an escape than simply a way of protecting herself while working on a personal identity that goes beyond 'dutiful daughter'.

Work can, however, be an unhealthy escape for some. Work addiction is a socially acceptable addiction that can slowly but inevitably kill, both physically and psychologically. In *Work Addiction* Bryan Robinson writes that while those addicted to work have symptoms similar to those of alcoholics, they are not so aware of their addiction because overwork is something that society rewards. People overwork, Robinson tells us, to try to fill a void within themselves.[5]

It is this void that perpetuates the feelings of loneliness. Where individuals have grown up with a poor self-concept and low self-worth they often experience an emptiness, a void, that can't be filled by work or any other activity.

All the same, they try harder and harder, hoping that somehow extra effort will make all the difference. All that will make a difference, though, is a healthier, more expanded sense of self.

Promoted to loneliness
For one man, it came as a complete surprise that his source of loneliness was a promotion.

I used to be one of the boys. I never imagined things would change so drastically when I became manager. Somehow, perhaps naively, I thought it would be much the same. But I find now they don't talk to me in the same way and conversations sometimes stop when I walk into the tea room. I would have to admit to feeling terribly lonely at work!

For this man, work had long provided him with a social network of support and comradeship, all of which seemed to evaporate when he took on his new position. He has to deal with the perceptions and attitudes of his colleagues, which now put him in a different class from them. His promotion means a better financial future, but a less satisfactory relationship with his colleagues — and that means loneliness at work.

Here is the irony of promotion: for many of us who achieve what we've aimed for it can be a hollow victory because feelings of alienation and loneliness might be lying in wait for us.

Executives may be particularly at risk of social alienation because their position requires their remaining aloof to some degree. Their role is to be strong and to make decisions about those things that affect employees' lives — their salaries and promotions, and restructuring of the organisation, for example.

With the responsibilities they have in the workplace, they may well neglect other areas of their lives: the result is often a deeper and deeper feeling of isolation as they come to terms with the fact that they have for so long believed in the myth that to be at the top was the ultimate and most fulfilling achievement.

What is often overlooked in relation to role change in the workplace is the need to change some attitudes, values and behaviour to fit the new position. Whether we are conscious of it or not, we do have expectations of certain positions within our workplace: our co-workers may, in turn, have differing expectations. If we take on one of those positions we may be faced with mixed messages about what is required, especially when no specific job description is provided. As a result we may feel alienated from our co-workers, anxious and unsure about how to best satisfy the job requirements. Ideally upper management will see the need for clear and detailed job specification, especially in times of great change and movement.

Emotional isolation

There are some personality traits that can contribute to emotional isolation within the context of work, apart from the cultural forces that include the value of independence, which we will discuss later on. While these personality traits may be most often associated with executives, they can be seen anywhere within the corporate hierarchy.

The first of these traits involves an attempt to appear completely self-sufficient and independent of anyone else. The problem is that this approach leads to a lack of close relationships at either a personal or a professional level so that in times of need there is no other person available. The type of person developing this trait is to be distinguished from those self-reliant people who tend to have a strong support network to depend on when the need is there. The fact that the network is in place is what allows these people to behave in an autonomous way.

Another of the traits contributing to emotional isolation and commonly seen in the workplace is a type of defensiveness that involves interactions that are either aggressive and controlling, or else submissive and non-assertive. Such defensiveness serves to alienate other people. The alternative involves a response that reflects responsibility, control, openness and some choice.

The consequences of emotional isolation can be a variety of symptoms, among which are feelings of depression, and burnout. While executives and managers may be more prone to these, they can happen anywhere within the organisation.

The value of team-building and teamwork is now being more widely acknowledged and promoted: they can alleviate to a large extent the problems of emotional isolation and loneliness in the workplace. Personal support networks, if they can be established and maintained, are also very useful, as is the provision of opportunities for employees to seek help when they are feeling isolated or alienated.

THE MYTH OF INDEPENDENCE

Here is a strong culturally based myth that has implications for all aspects of our lives, but perhaps more especially the workplace. This may be because it is an aspect of the work-mask already mentioned and it has been named as one of the forces contributing to emotional isolation for those who move into executive positions.

But it applies to us all, and it represents one of those areas in which many of us have continuing internal conflict: essentially, to stand on one's own feet and operate completely as an individual or else to depend on others and work together as a team. Either choice can leave us feeling lonely if we do not make it from a position of internal strength and commitment.

The early years

One of the many goals for most parents is to help their children develop into independent young people who will be able to function well in the world. It is natural that we want our children to enjoy the ability to do this, but there is another dimension. To a large extent, our children's independence means in turn our own independence, our own opportunity to step back and watch them fly and to attend to our own interests and other commitments.

Independence is something we all strive for, from toddlerhood to adulthood. From the age of around two, we become more and more aware of our own individuality and begin to express a powerful need to define and assert ourselves. During this process of self-discovery, however, we are made aware, by the adults around us, that we must be conscious of the needs of others. It might be charming at three years of age, for example, that we romp and roll at great speed and at great volume in the back-yard, but it becomes clear that to do the same thing on the floor of the supermarket or when visiting family friends who entertain us in a small, gardenless unit is simply not acceptable.

The ensuing couple of years will see us becoming less egocentric and more able to judge when we need to depend on others and when we can be independent. Ideally, the maturation process during early and middle childhood, and later through adolescence and early adulthood, involves a steady development of this ability to assess just when independence is appropriate and, in fact, necessary.

However, what has been termed the 'struggle for independence' is aptly named: it is indeed a struggle to maintain a sense of self in relation to others while establishing one's individual self separate from those same others. This is even more difficult if the struggle is either thwarted, or avoided by young people being pushed into it before they are ready.

Having independence foisted upon them prematurely can lead to feelings of insecurity and loneliness in young people, as several studies have indicated.[6] On the other hand, the same feelings result from an over-dependence on parents. The development of personal identity, and of the varieties of social relationships with peers of both sexes, can suffer where there is a prolonged attachment to parents.

A struggle for identity

The case of the 'foreclosed identity' is an example of the undermining of a young person's struggle for a genuine identity that is self-evolved: the foreclosed identity has been channelled into a path chosen mainly by others, and most usually by parents.

The price for the adolescents who fall into line is the surrender of the opportunity to explore and discover for themselves, and to make their own decisions with all the concomitant pitfalls. It could be supposed that where there has been no natural development of bonds, of personal enthusiasms, or of decision-making processes, life would seem meaningless and a deep, soul-hungry loneliness would result.

Francis sees herself as falling into this category.

At the time I asked no questions: what my mother suggested for me I did, although I realise now that she put things forward as 'suggestions' when really it was clear that there was no other choice. Options were not discussed. I even followed the career path she thought suited me best — mind you, there's nothing wrong with parents giving guidance, it's just that some guidance is actually a narrowed, blinkered path down a one-way passage, with no chance of glancing across to what other paths there might be.

It was not until she reached thirty years of age and had a couple of children of her own that Francis took real notice. She says now:

> I know that everyone takes stock of their life and the road they've taken at some stage, and I have done that since then, but at the time my passivity hit me with force, if that's possible! I felt deeply alone despite what seemed to be a quite good relationship with my partner, although subsequently that needed an overhaul. I suppose the main problem was that I had no idea how I'd arrived where I was: with that job, with that mate, with kids. None of it seemed to have anything to do with me, and I felt detached in a way, removed from my own life, and so lonely.

It has been almost ten years since Francis's revelation, and while she still experiences periods of deep loneliness, it has never been, to use her own words, 'as soul-numbing'. Using that well-developed skill of hers of observing in a detached manner has allowed her to pinpoint what works for her and what is not to her own taste. Essential to the process has been practice in making decisions, wise or not, and in exploring possibilities, and then taking responsibility for outcomes.

No-one can deny the value of this process for human beings of any age. In fact no-one can deny the importance of the development of a healthy independence of which taking responsibility is a part.

Breaking free

History, for men anyway, has hailed the concept of independence, although taking responsibility has not always been a priority. Men have been lauded for their independence, their related bravery and audacity and sense of adventure. On the other hand, in the past, women who have dipped into the waters of independence have been subject, usually both covertly and overtly, to criticism and suspicion and judgement.

Fortunately for both genders, life is different now. Brave battles have ensured widespread changes in the Western world that have included just and appropriate freedom for those whose identities have been shackled or denied.

The push for marginalised groups along with the young of our culture to attain independence has a sound basis: all human beings have the right to be acknowledged for the individuals they are, and for that to come about they need to stand on their own in the sun and out of the shadows created by others. To be independent means, literally, not to be dependent on anyone else, either to protect, hide or define one in any way.

On the basis of this thinking there is no arguing that independence is a good thing: however, philosophers and historians tell us that it has not always been that individuals struggle for the sort of independence we know and desire, and the personal identity that we regard as just as important.

Various writers, notably psychoanalyst Erich Fromm,[7] argue that it is only since the Middle Ages and the Renaissance that people have developed a sense of their own individuality. Norbert Elias, for example, writes that we have seen a gradual but vast change in the balance between what he refers to as 'we-identity' and 'I-identity'. He points out that while people used to belong to a certain group for the term of their lives, so that their I-identity was linked to their we-identity, which was often the more powerful, over time 'the pendulum swung to the opposite extreme. The we-identity of people, though it certainly always remained present, was now often overshadowed or concealed in consciousness by their I-identity.'[8]

Elias credits Descartes with the beginnings of the shift of emphasis because of his famed assertion 'Cogito, ergo sum' (I think, therefore I am). At that time it was heredity that tended to group people and so determined their identity to a large extent. From royalty and nobility, with their family trees, to peasants who were associated with the land, every individual identified with a group.

This we-identity disappeared as an individual was engaged in thinking and the 'I' became the dominating principle. One's own thought, one's own reason, became the only real thing, all that was free of illusion. 'This form of I-identity,' Elias writes, 'the perception of one's own person as a we-less I, has spread wide and deep since then.'[9]

This 'we-less I' is the ultimate independent and the totally self-sufficient. It is the person who may well put the pursuit and attainment of individualism above most else. It is a person highly admired by much of Western society. The dynamic that results from the value placed on independence and self-sufficiency is one that emphasises the individual and separates individual from group.

The myth

The myth of independence rests on the concept that to be truly independent is to be omnipotent, in need of no-one either in a physical or psychological sense. Movie heroes of the past have perpetuated the myth, with solitary, self-sufficient characters living seemingly fulfilled lives on their own and on the move.

For experts in relationships, these characters are the archetypes of those who are unable to form lasting, meaningful relationships with others: contrary to their image, these are deeply fearful people, fearful of closeness, unsure of what it means to be intimate with another person, unsure of what it means to know oneself to any degree. Because of all these things, they remain removed from genuine contact with other human beings. All the same, their image is an attractive one, especially in a culture that tends to encourage independence.

However, independence is not a goal in all cultures: a study[10] in 1980 of 160 000 working people in sixty countries found that while Westerners regard independence and individualism highly, the Oriental cultures place far less importance on these values. For them, the group and the family system are highly prized so that attachment is the common process, rather than separation.

Because we all know that attachment is related to bonding while separation can lead to emotional isolation and loneliness, it would be tempting to embrace wholeheartedly this particular attitude to the group and the family.

However, to regard this latter view as a solution to human and social problems is to overlook the human need to explore and to reach for self-realisation. Traditionally, where the group is the dominant entity, the individual is forced into a position of subordination to group, inhibition of all individualistic behaviour, and limiting of freedom to move beyond the needs and requirements of the group.

It would seem, superficially at least, that the Western culture and the Oriental culture represent, respectively, the 'I-identity' and the 'we-identity' of earlier discussion.

With regard to loneliness, the emotional isolation of those who distance themselves from others in the mistaken belief that they are being self-sufficient is naturally a forerunner to a lonely existence. And for those feeling trapped in a group state, with no sense of individual self, loneliness can be excruciating, with people all around and available, but an underdeveloped ability to relate as an individual.

The common factor in these situations is the culturally based force, either for individualism at any cost or the group at any cost. The greatest cost of all is that we trade our souls to conform to what is required of us: but awareness is our greatest tool, and once we recognise the trap, the challenge is to work our selves free of the cultural forces so as to make choices based on our own needs and inclinations.

Healing the lonely body

10

THE WOUNDED BODY
The loneliness of grief

Grief is the normal response to loss and is a necessary process because it allows healing to take place. Feelings of grief have very real characteristics: physical reactions such as sleeplessness, loss of appetite, digestive disturbances and shortness of breath, a sense of emptiness and tension, exhaustion and distance from other people, preoccupation at times with whoever or whatever has been lost, guilt over what we could have done but didn't, and a sense of restlessness and aimlessness together with a lack of motivation to do much at all.

We human beings go to some lengths to protect ourselves from the painful feelings of loss. Towards the end of World War II, the 'anticipatory grief reaction' was described. It referred to what sometimes happened during times of long separation such as wartime, when the person remaining worked through the grief process as if the absent person had died. Complications arose when that person returned because the grief work had been so effectively carried out that the partner at home had detached from the absent one and now had little or no feeling for them.

Bereavement, like any loss, can trigger deep feelings of loneliness. Losing an intimate means the severing of a bond, the sudden loss of everyday companionship and sustenance. Relationship can play an integral part in the health of an individual, especially when that relationship provides love, care and support. Broken ties can result in broken bodies: bodies racked by heart disease, cancer, or other illnesses.

The effects of bereavement are widely documented: for example, one study[1] revealed that, during the first year of bereavement, there was a sevenfold increase in the death rate for surviving close relatives. On the biological level, an Australian study was one of the first to show that bereavement may be followed by defective functioning of the immune system in the grieving spouse.[2]

Losing a mate in particular can be devastating, especially if, as has been suggested,[3] the two have worked together as a single entity at some level. It seems that in these cases there is 'a literal union of the two psyches that operates in spite of physical separation. It is possible that this felt sense of union sets the stage for catastrophic mind–body effects when either husband or wife dies.'[4]

While we commonly think of grief in terms of bereavement only, it can be experienced in many other contexts. The loss of status, or of possessions, or of a job, can lead to feelings of grief, as can developmental change. Pre-adolescent children, for example, will sometimes even become mildly depressed over what they see as the impending loss of childhood.

Many young adults in their final year of school, while pleased to have that part of their life almost at an end, experience some grief at that very ending. Mothers know the grief, along with the joy, associated with growing children — the last of breastfeeding, the first day of school.

The range of feelings that accompany any changes are as much due to the sense of loss as to the fear of new responsibilities and commitment, or simply a new way of being, lying ahead.

Whatever the cause of the grief may be, there is often a deep sense of loneliness associated with it. As medical practitioners are discovering more and more frequently, feelings of isolation, alienation and loneliness can have profound effects on the health of an individual.

The mind–body connection

The physical consequences of loneliness bear some enquiry. Let's take a look at the bigger picture.

One of the most difficult problems that philosophers and scientists of the Western tradition have had to tackle is the one regarding the mind–body connection. How does the interaction between thought and atoms of the physical body take place? How can feeling lonely affect the way our body works?

No-one knows exactly, and the theorising goes on. Yet there is no doubt that changes of a biochemical nature take place in response to our perceptions and our emotions: there is plenty of clinical proof, though most of us know from first-hand experience that it is so.

Changes in the autonomic nervous system — a sudden fall in blood pressure, or slowing down of the heart, or dilation of arteries — can all follow the announcement of bad news, for example.

There is considerable documentation on the suppression of the immune system in response to stress, too: as we've noted already, spouses who have lost their partners can suffer fatal illnesses within the first year of bereavement because their immune cells are not protecting them as they normally would.

Physiological changes can occur in response to positive emotions as well: good news, falling in love, feeling optimistic and positive about the future can all have very beneficial effects on our overall health.

Despite all the evidence to indicate correlations between physical changes and the experience of thoughts and emotions — whether negative or positive — we still do not understand how they happen, but only that they do happen.

In considering the 'how' of the mind–body connection, it is probable that we need a leap in understanding to a new paradigm. There may be a third dimension, as yet undetermined, which explains the relation between mind and body, or matter. A leading theoretical physicist, David Bohm, has suggested that this third thing, this thing that explains the whole mind–body connection and all the results that clinicians have been reporting for some time, may be meaning. He has said that he would like to turn our minds to a new way of thinking '... consistent with modern physics, that does not divide mind from matter or subject from object ... Meaning, which is simultaneously mental and physical, can serve as the link or bridge between realms ...'[5]

It is as if mind and body are the two poles of a magnet and meaning is the magnetic field: although each appears to be a separate entity, each only exists in the context of the others. The three — mind, body, meaning — form one whole.

For those who concur with this view, disease and illness have a message. If we are able to understand the meaning behind a physical condition we may change the course of it one way or another or at least apply the understanding to our life.

This makes sense if we imagine that the meaning resides in the body: it isn't that our mind interprets an event and 'tells' our body, but that meanings are carried in our physical body 'by chemical and electrical processes into the brain and the rest of the nervous system, where they are apprehended at higher and higher intellectual and emotional levels of meaning'.[6]

Here is an example of extracting meaning from illness: when I came down with a 'flu virus a little while ago, the overwhelming feeling was that I was drowning. It was similar to the feeling of being caught by a wave and struggling to the surface to gasp for air. The drowning sensation rang a clear bell for me: I had recently been under stress to complete some work, to attend to the needs of my family and various other people in my life, and to handle some financial matters I had promised some others to do. Waves of panic would hit, most usually in the middle of the night when I felt least able to tackle the tasks at hand. The 'meaning' of my illness was very clear: while recovering I gave some deep thought as to how I could prioritise and delegate, two skills that do not come easily to me. I subsequently tried putting them more and more into practice.

Meaning can vary vastly from one of us to another. Carl Jung put special emphasis on individual interpretation, especially with respect to dreams. He insisted that they have meaning only within the context of an individual's own life: a dictionary of dream meanings, for example, makes the assumption that we all think the same way, perceive experiences in the same way, derive the same meaning from everything around us.

My dream of being in the garden pulling out weeds and your dream of being in your garden pulling out weeds may seem to have the same content, but my meaning and your meaning are possibly quite, quite different. Meaning is an excitingly individual thing. To assume these dreams mean the same thing to us both is to make us machines that respond equally to the same stimuli or input.

The meaning of alone

The statistics that tell us of the premature deaths of those who live alone and of those recently bereaved may blind us to the fact that, while social isolation and personal loss can be devastating, there are many people who survive both quite healthily. In fact, many in these situations live long, happy, productive and satisfying lives. What is of fundamental importance here is the meaning that being alone holds for each of us.

If aloneness has for us always been associated with abandonment, rejection and isolation, then to find ourselves alone would be a most unpleasant and possibly terrifying experience. If aloneness is perceived by us as something that happens to friendless, unfriendly, cold people, then we may begin to see ourselves in the same way, and it wouldn't be long before self-loathing set in. Being alone would mean to be lonely. In this case, the meaning we attach to being alone is what is destructive to us, rather than the state of aloneness itself.

If, on the other hand, aloneness holds a great attraction to us, if we were always encouraged to enjoy our own company as well as that of friends when appropriate and to find interests we could pursue on our own, then to be left alone would not be so distressing. We may have to cope with bereavement, but the aftermath of being alone would not be a devastating consequence. We may feel lonely occasionally, but we would not expect it as a necessary result of being alone. Our meaning of alone would help us at this time to come to terms with our life situation.

In a Californian study[7] involving 7000 healthy people, women who felt socially isolated had a much greater chance than their counterparts of developing and dying from cancer. It was not the actual number of social contacts that mattered to these women, but rather how they felt with respect to aloneness. If women felt isolated, but had many social contacts, they had 2.4 times the risk of dying from cancer (of the breast, uterus and ovaries), whereas if they not only felt isolated but also had very few social contacts, then they had five times the risk of dying from these cancers.

What this emphasises is the role of meaning in our lives, and therefore the role of meaning in the health of our bodies. This concept takes us far beyond the old notion of our bodies as machines.

THE HEALING PHENOMENON

In light of the fact that feelings of loneliness, isolation and alienation can have serious effects on the health of the body, let's consider how we can heal the lonely body.

It may require that we listen carefully to our bodies and what they are telling us about their needs, rather than relying on our beliefs and attitudes to inform us; it may require us to learn new techniques in handling the thoughts we have about feeling lonely which can wear away at the immune system; it may require that we think about how to feed our bodies sensually; and it may require that we put more emphasis on our own ability to avoid the pain of loneliness, or to use it to our advantage in growing and developing as human beings.

Dealing with feelings

Tuning in to our bodies, especially if we are not in the habit of doing it, can have some very surprising results. For one thing, we may suddenly become aware of feelings that we haven't noticed before.

Despite our awareness of the importance of really feeling and expressing our emotions, the truth for most of us is that we simply don't know how to manage our emotions at all. That's partly because we often don't recognise what we're feeling anyway, except for a vaguely uncomfortable sense that makes us irritable and argumentative, or else drives us to withdrawal and escape.

Simple as it seems, the most important step in managing emotions is to recognise them in the first place. If in a quiet moment I close my eyes and visualise a situation, real or imagined, that makes me feel lonely and isolated, I can feel the emotions churn in my body. Where? It varies from one individual to another.

For example, for some the feeling of loneliness may manifest itself as an emptiness in the pit of the stomach; for others it may be a feeling akin to helplessness and powerlessness that rises slowly in the throat looking for vocal expression; for others again it may be a sense of panic that swirls away in the stomach.

According to one study, the feelings most often reported by people who label themselves 'lonely' are sadness, depression, boredom, self-pity, and longing to be with one special person.[8]

In this same study, four main types of feelings emerged. The first of these was desperation, which was characterised by feelings of panic, fear and abandonment and often followed the breaking of a relationship. Impatient boredom — feeling bored, angry, and restless — was more common to younger people and was associated with social isolation. Depression (feeling sad, empty and isolated), and self-deprecation (feeling ashamed and insecure), were both seen as reactions to loneliness, and particularly a prolonged experience of loneliness.

While all feelings and emotions are valid experiences for us, and we have the freedom to express them, we may need some guidance in dealing with them.

At this point, let me tell you of an incident that demonstrated to me something very interesting about emotions. Some years ago, when I was participating in counselling training with a group of people, one of the group was telling the leader about a particular fear he was experiencing. As he talked about it, he began to shake quite violently, and his eyes opened wide as he stuttered about his terror. Quietly, the leader took his hand and said: 'Imagine that what you are feeling at the moment is excitement. Imagine that you actually feeling excited about this situation — there is part of you really looking forward to being there.' The man stopped shaking, his eyes took on a more normal appearance and he began to smile. 'How does it feel now?' the leader asked. 'I feel great,' the man replied, and settled back into his chair for the next session.

What happened here was that the leader reframed a situation: she helped change the man's perception of the situation. She helped him with a new meaning, and so changed his response to the thought of the upcoming event.

Over the years I have tried this technique many times on myself and on others. It is very effective, but it should only be used in certain circumstances. The danger with the method is that strong feelings can be denied. There are times when it is healthy to be fearful, for example: fear is the emotion that is presenting itself and to try reframing it may be unwise because it will resurface before long in a possibly destructive way. Fear may be telling us to be cautious and to take care of ourselves. We need to listen to it when it is appropriate.

Other emotions present themselves to be noticed and listened to as well: each has its own meaning for us and its own course of action.

How do we know when to reframe an emotion? Getting to know ourselves more and more thoroughly is essential, because we begin to recognise when it is appropriate to reframe and when it is a good idea to stay with the emotion and its messages. Once we know ourselves better, we can pass on a feeling too: for example, we can ask ourselves whether the anger or fear or anxiety we are feeling is all that constructive for us at present, and whether, if we let it go, we might be doing ourselves some good. Letting a feeling go when it might be destructive for us is quite different from denying our feelings. It is a mature and healthful decision to make when holding on to an emotion can simply wear us down and wear us out.

Being able to reframe, to change the meaning of a situation, is particularly valuable for people who are prone to feeling lonely. By all means, we should go ahead and feel lonely if we choose to — there is much for each of us to learn in our times of loneliness, and to reflect deeply when we are feeling lonely in the world can even be a spiritual experience. However, if feeling lonely is a regular and unwanted experience, then examining the meaning of loneliness for us would be fruitful.

One woman who found loneliness a frequent visitor said:

It was hard to break out of the cycle of loneliness–sadness–helplessness–self-pity–more loneliness ... I was getting more depressed and my work was suffering, and I had stopped contacting my friends because I felt so uninspiring to be with.

Then I made a decision. I don't even know what made me do it, although someone told me once that when something hurts enough we do something about it! Maybe that's what it was. I called a couple of friends and arranged a weekend away with them, even though it was the last thing I felt like at the time. I realised how effortless it is to be lonely sometimes — you just sit around at night thinking about how awful things are instead of choosing action.

It's unfair to generalise, I suppose, but I do think that people who are lonely get themselves into a habit — the way I did. The silly thing is that it isn't impossible to climb out of the hole. I still feel lonely occasionally, but I don't let myself dwell on it. I see it as a normal feeling that comes and goes, and I get on with other things. It's worked for me.

For this woman, loneliness changed from being a hole of helplessness to 'a normal feeling that comes and goes'. She recognised that allowing herself to wallow in lonely feelings kept her from moving out towards others, perhaps taking risks, and living a fuller and more satisfying life. It isn't always this simple but moving away from constant loneliness is often just a matter of making a choice.

The use of mindfulness

Making such a choice is easier for us when we know ourselves and our deepest feelings quite well. How can we achieve this state of knowing? One way involves stepping back from our normal mode of operating.

Notice how, whether you are alone or in the company of other people, your mind is given to endless chatter: you can hold whole conversations in your head without uttering a single word, and work yourself into a lather by dwelling on what should be that isn't, or what has been done that shouldn't have been done.

Mind-chatter can leave us utterly exhausted, especially if it involves a stirring up of emotions. If we are feeling lonely, we can talk and talk at ourselves in our heads, telling ourselves what is wrong with us that we don't feel differently, and feeling envious of others who don't seem to be experiencing such painful loneliness.

The voice up there in the head can drive us to distraction, which is literally what it does. There is an alternative to mind chatter, though, but it does take conscious effort and determination.

Mindfulness is the 'activity of the mind that can wake us from our "sleep" and allow us to experience and participate in the pulsating, ever-changing, sensuous vitality of the here and now'. It involves observing our experiences, both inner and outer, while they are happening in the present moment. Rather than seeing and experiencing what is going on in our minds, mindfulness allows us 'to settle down, to quiet, to see and experience what is happening in our lives'.[9]

Solitude is essential to mindfulness, which explains why so few pursue its rewards. Being alone — being in solitude — can be threatening to many of us in our world of endless activity and sound and other sensory input. To be away from all these distractions can feel empty and lifeless. Paradoxically, solitude can lead us back to a full, vital life.

How does mindfulness work? By bringing our attention to the here and now, by enjoying what is in the present and taking in the full sensuous pleasure of that.

We have been trained, by and large, to believe that to enjoy life to the full we need many others around us. While there is no doubt that we have a need for social contact and for a network of friends — the size of the network varies from one of us to another — what the social contact can do is to mask the other need we have, which is to enjoy the self, to revel in our own company, and to enjoy the sensuality of life on our own.

I can remember cleaning up after a meal once with a friend who practises mindfulness. It was a joy to be with him as he washed the cups and cutlery and dishes with such care and focused attention. He had prepared and cooked the dinner earlier with the same mindfulness. What is, for most of us, a ritual we engage in night after night, became a sort of dance, and by the end of the evening we were all feeling relaxed and refreshed after an experience that still sings in my memory.

Mindfulness requires dedication and practice: it involves detaching from the chaos of mind-chatter and focusing our attention until our mind and body are still. It is then that we move into a state of reflection, and then gradually to meditation where there is a sense of emptiness of the best sort, a sense of peace and serenity. Meditation 'releases the inner physician by quieting the mind so that the body's own inner wisdom can be heard ...'[10] and the consequence is that we are better able to listen to ourselves and to make the best decisions for ourselves too.

Blaise Pascal wrote that all of our miseries are the result of our inability to be alone and quiet. Perhaps he was right, especially regarding the misery of loneliness. To be mindful and to meditate when we are feeling lonely is to take responsibility by looking inwards to listen to our inner wisdom. The result is that we move beyond the feeling state, which is uncomfortable and comfortless, to a state of peace and tranquillity, the place of the soul.

THE POWER OF TOUCH
Touching for healing
Every true healer understands the magical power of touch. Where words are inadequate, a touch says everything. Where

181

thoughts and feelings are begging to be heard but too deeply felt to express, a touch can connect and reassure. Where joy is experienced, it is intensified by touch.

Touching is one of our most basic needs. Even the rational, cerebral world of scientific research has demonstrated that. Baby monkeys deprived of touch soon die after birth, and for others given the choice of a surrogate mother that is soft and warm and one that is made of wire mesh but provides food, the one that gives tactile comfort is preferred over the one providing food alone.

In the world of primates, tactile communication plays a large part. Mothers carry their young for some time, and there is a lot of contact with other group members too. They tend to sit and sleep together closely, nuzzle and pat each other, and grooming is most important, as much for the contact involved as to keep the body clean.

On the human front, babies who are not fondled, cuddled, handled, played with, simply do not survive, and in cases where the touching is limited, both physical and psychological development are seriously impaired. So convinced are many sociologists and others that large amounts of tactile contact are essential to the developing infant, that they state that impersonal childrearing practices — early separation from the mother, the use of bottles, blankets, pacifiers, prams and other objects to keep parent and child apart, the time-tabling of feeds, and so on — produce adults who lead lonely, isolated lives and look to the materialistic world to satisfy them.

In his celebrated book *Touching: The Human Significance of the Skin*, Ashley Montagu explores a range of intercultural studies on the importance of touching. 'The evidence ... suggests that adequate tactile satisfaction during infancy and childhood is of fundamental importance for the subsequent healthy behavioural development of the individual.'[11] He recommends that we parents of the Western world express our affection for each other and for our children more openly than we have before. It is action that communicates warmth and caring and involvement that we all need, Montagu argues.

Given the proven importance of touch, it is remarkable that, in our culture, we have been so restrained in its use. Even babies who are fondled very much in infancy are touched less and less as they grow, so that by puberty the amount of tactile contact these human beings receive has diminished to almost nothing. Little wonder, then, that at some stage the act of communication that allows most physical contact — sexual intercourse — is seen as the only way to satisfy our very deep needs.

All that needs to be expressed, but cannot be verbalised, all the anxieties and uncertainties of living, along with the pleasures and the joy, are directed into the sexual act so that, rather than being a deeply satisfying and unifying contact, it can become a source of frustration and disappointment.

More than twenty years ago, when I first started to teach young teenagers, a more experienced teacher who was much loved and respected by every student, shared her secret with me. 'When they file into the room for a lesson,' she told me, 'I always stand at the door and I make sure to make contact with each one of them. The slightest touch makes a difference. I notice how much they calm down, and besides that, they feel personally welcomed by me.'

In moving towards another person and touching them, we disregard superficial barriers that keep us firmly individuals and definitely separate. To touch is certainly to risk. There is in touch the underlying dimension of trust. When I talk to you I can remain hidden despite my possible facility with words or your interested and sensitive questioning. But when we touch we are both vulnerable.

Put your arm gently around someone who is struggling to maintain composure and the floodgates burst. In touch is the power to let loose those deeply held emotions, long held prisoner. How interesting that we use the word 'feeling' to mean both emotion and touching — here is proof of how closely bound they are.

As our society has become more and more technologically orientated, our need for touch from other human beings has increased as well. While the information/technology age continues to evolve, the 'personal, high-touch corollary develops as a counter to this trend, to satisfy human needs in social, emotional and spiritual areas of life'.[12]

The healing power of animals

It seems that our blood pressure can drop quite dramatically when we reach out to stroke and pat our pet. We drop our voices, speak gently and feel quite comfortable uttering nonsense syllables that we could speak to no other human being.

I have witnessed the amazing effect of our dog Kaa on my own family and various visitors to our home. When someone is feeling tired, strung out or just a little bit down, Kaa is a wonderful companion: she sits close and seems to tune in to the mood of the moment. People who in most situations can be quite formal will start to say sweet doggy-nothings to her, and I can remember my delight in watching one particular friend — a quiet, reserved man — throwing a stick to her and becoming very excited by her response. He told me:

> You can act like a child when you are with your pet. You wouldn't dare do that in public with another person, and besides, other people have their own agendas and all communication reflects that. Animals are totally accepting and non-judgemental — they don't regard you as strange if you get down on all fours and bark or miaow a little!

Here lies the healing power of animals — they can make good companions and they allow us to let loose the wild little child within us who was well-socialised early but needs to have a romp at least every now and then. Animals also enjoy being patted and stroked, both of which can satisfy some of our own needs for touch.

Filling our senses

Having said all this, it is important to point out that our needs for touch do vary considerably, and that there are certainly ways to satisfy the need even when we are alone and lack companionship.

Indiscriminate hugging may fill a momentary need, but it can leave us feeling lonelier than ever in the long run. Many people make the mistake of believing that it is only in a romantic relationship that such a need can be met, and plunge into this sort of relationship without being aware of the pitfalls of such a move. Unless we can ourselves satisfy the need for touch, or for any other sense for that matter, looking to another to fill it can lead to deep disappointment.

Many of us spend enormous amounts of time looking for the right person who understands us, or else regretting our choice of mate because our needs are not being met: but we tend not to question ourselves or to look very deeply within to find out why we are not being satisfied. As one writer puts it:

> There is a difference between the healthy desire to share the intimacy and companionship of another and the unhealthy search for relationship as an antidote to the anxiety and pain of loneliness. The latter can only be resolved by first developing a healthy relationship with oneself.[13]

How can we develop a healthy relationship with ourselves? We can begin by learning to fill our own senses.

In terms of tactile contact, there are a number of ways that we can enjoy touch without being in a partnership. Treating ourselves to a regular massage, for example, satisfies the need for touch along with a few side-benefits: it can iron out stress and, while relaxing us, can leave our bodies feeling more alive than ever.

We can become touchers if we aren't already: we can make sure to touch or hug our friends and our family members. We can delight the child within us all by spending time with children, being open to their openness and reciprocating their ease with touch. And we can make love to ourselves, exploring our bodies with the sensitivity and care that the most wonderful and understanding of lovers would.

These are some of the ways we can enjoy the sense of touch without involving an intimate partner, but we can also consider putting more effort into our other senses so that our need for touch is not so intense. The intensity of the need always seems greatest when we are alone and with what seems no hope of company. This is the time when planned strategies can be brought into action: we can think ahead of time, when we are feeling even relatively satisfied with life, about the things that bring us most pleasure.

Sitting under an umbrella outside a café and sipping good coffee is a favourite pastime of mine: I enjoy the taste and smell of the coffee, I enjoy watching the people moving back and forth or sitting at the other tables, and I enjoy hearing the chatter around me and knowing that I don't have to respond.

A walk in the park, a long hike, a visit to the art gallery, a night at a concert, a good book, a new recording of a loved classic … The ways to fill our senses are infinite, if only we choose to enjoy ourselves without feeling the need to have someone by our side.

Reclaiming
wholeness

11

OUR ESTRANGEMENT
Alienation from nature

There was a time when we human beings were intimately related to our food, our shelter and our clothes because we were directly involved in producing them, both for our families and for our communities.

Those days are long since gone and we are far removed from this primary participation which satisfied some basic needs: not only were we providing food and shelter, but our contact with others was regular and it was meaningful too, in the sense that goals were met while working closely side by side.[1]

These days we live in a mechanised society as consumers rather than as producers. Philosopher Rollo May talks of our being estranged from nature and the sense of despair we feel but find difficult to express, about our lack of relationship with the natural world, which includes our own body. Part of the difficulty has to do with division of labour and specialisation.

It was not so long ago in terms of centuries that people had an almost complete knowledge of the world that was immediately around them. These days, however, each of us knows a tinier and tinier percentage of the total knowledge being accumulated by human beings.

The consequence is a lack of an overall view of the world and its workings and, instead, extreme specialisation to the exclusion eventually of even quite closely related fields.[2] What meaning can there be in this existence? Cut off more and more from our neighbours, we find ourselves isolated and even alienated.

This estrangement from nature manifests itself in almost all our everyday activities: we house ourselves in modern, often highly technologised buildings, we eat food that is all but chewed and digested for us, we travel in little capsules on four wheels that keep us protected from the teeming masses outside, we work in air-conditioned offices dressed in clothing stitched up to impress, we spend weekends in a spin of activity to avoid boredom and to ensure a good time.

Returning to those former days of attending to basics with co-operative effort may not be a viable solution to the current problem that this scenario reveals. But while we might argue that much about life today is preferable to the pre-industrial way of living, at the same time we have not found a way to replicate the aspect that best served us: the contact with nature, the contact with others, and, most importantly, the deep contact with ourselves.

Lack of connection in an impersonal society

Ashley Montagu, writing about the impersonality of life in the Western world, tells that we have become strangers to each other, 'faceless figures in a crowded landscape and suffering deep loneliness'.[3] This comes from *Touching: The Human Significance of the Skin*, but its meaning goes beyond mere physical touch. We are largely a group of out-of-touch people, in all senses of the expression.

As our lives have become increasingly sophisticated, we have become increasingly distanced from each other, anonymous members of a society that pushes on regardless, refining technology and emphasising economic advancement. We can run the race or we can pull out, but either choice takes its toll.

If we choose to run the race we may find that we continue to lose touch with basics: in fact we may find out too late, when we discover ourselves so far from base camp that it is almost impossible to pick our way back even if we wanted to. Running the race, deciding to compete, means playing the same game as everyone else, and that usually means developing a mask[4] that is recognised on the field. It may mean a good deal of inauthenticity, as we take on the qualities which are necessary to survive but which do not resonate with our core self.

If we choose not to run the race, there are some other difficult decisions to make: How do we be in the world? What do we give up and what do we persevere with? Who is the 'me' that I present to the world? Am I out of touch with what is real and true but not aware of it? What do I keep and what do I discard in order to maintain my relationship with the natural world which includes my own body?

'Only connect', urged E. M. Forster in his novel *Howards End*.[5] Certainly connection is what is missing in a disengaged, impersonal society. Lack of connection is what leaves us feeling emotionally isolated, utterly lonely and, in some cases, hostile and cynical towards a world that marginalises and abuses.

For some people, the situation becomes paradoxical: to encourage closeness and intimacy with others, they announce their specialness and therefore their right to be loved and respected. 'I am really something', they say, or words to that effect. 'Pay attention to me, like me and love me and respect me', desperate words sure to deter the kindest acquaintance.

It is sadly ironic that, in trying to establish connection with others, we can further isolate ourselves by setting ourselves apart. To be reconnected we need have no pretensions, no claims to fame or special treatment. We need be only our humble, authentic selves. Conditioned and caught up in the worldly whirl as we are, this is no simple feat.

Overcoming separateness

Imagine being an infant once again. Cosy and warm we feel as our cheek rests against mother's breast. In the traditional view of symbiosis,[6] while we are one with her we are also at one with the entire universe, experiencing what has been referred to as 'union with being' and enjoying deep calm and satisfaction with what goes beyond the filling of a tiny stomach.

Time and again as children, as adolescents, as young adults, as middle-agers and in older age, we try to repeat that early time, making attempts to return to that blissful Garden of Eden where we are totally safe and accepted. Loneliness and emotional isolation are unknown there.

Exploring why it is that humans communicate, psychologist Erich Fromm suggests that part of being human is being aware of the self, and this means recognising that we are different from others and separate from them. The result, he says, is that we look for contact and unification with others. 'The deepest need of man, then,' he wrote in 'The Theory of Love', 'is the need to overcome his separateness, to leave the prison of his aloneness.'[7]

Isolation from others is most commonly considered when talk of being lonely surfaces. When feelings of loneliness tease, the briefest encounter with another human being can help enormously. Having lost contact with what is too difficult to name, sometimes simply the sight of other beings can be enough to remind us of our humanness and their doings can remind us of the extraordinary ordinariness of life. It can be strangely comforting and restorative.

But there are two other forms of isolation that can be just as devastating. The first is isolation from a higher force, the 'Other',[8] or God; the second is isolation from the inner self.

While isolation can be separated into three types to clarify the term and its expression, the three are interdependent and, some would argue, indistinguishable. If I am at peace with myself and at one with the core of my being, am I not then at one with my God, and am I not one with my friend and neighbour too? And, if I am experiencing unity with all of nature, in a Garden of Eden of sorts, am I not then necessarily at one with my sister and with myself as well?

To be at peace with ourselves can be a lifelong dream and goal. It requires that we totally accept who we are, which first of all necessitates knowing who we are. If we live constantly outside ourselves, as Rousseau suggested, knowing only how to live in the opinion of others, not ever daring to ask ourselves who we are, then it may be an impossible task.

If, because of early judgement from our caretakers, or the society that bred us, or our religion, we believe we have an imperfect self, we will keep ourselves hidden. In this way, who we are publicly and who we are privately are widely different, and the greater this discrepancy the greater the shame that we feel when we are alone with ourselves, and so the more lonely we feel.

Dean Ornish suggests that, to help us feel more connected to other people and to help us transcend our sense of separateness rather than continuing to feel alone and isolated, we turn our hearts to compassion and forgiveness. He suggests, too, that we refrain from judgement, which increases isolation and separation, because it emphasises our differences rather than our similarities.[9]

Judgement, together with an unforgiving attitude, keeps us locked in a defensive position: feeling self-righteous, we tend to make an island of ourselves, perhaps because we feel we ourselves may be under attack. The truth is that our 'enemy' resides more on the inside than on the outside, and while we isolate ourselves from outside attack we are in fact isolating ourselves from our *selves*. In John Milton's words 'Which way I fly is Hell; myself am Hell'.[10]

When we are determined to be right, we shut down any little voice that whispers 'Surrender', and close down our hearts. How else can we be but lonely when we isolate ourselves in this way?

> ... to the degree that we perceive ourselves as a part of the world rather than apart from it — connected and intimate rather than isolated and alone — then we can begin changing the self-destructive perceptions and the resulting behaviour patterns that leave us feeling even more lonely.[11]

This is not to say that we let other people walk all over us and that we must not defend ourselves in any way. On the contrary. Protecting ourselves is of utmost importance, but it requires a clarity of focus: as we've seen, protection can work against us when we put up barriers and operate in an inauthentic way — that is, a way that is not a true expression of who we are.

But we need to distinguish between this sort of protection that keeps us hidden and unreachable and the sort of protection that is healthy for the self, the sort that shuts out judgement and criticism. We need to protect ourselves as we would protect our young, with care and tenderness, together with a keen eye for what is good and what is not.

Loss of spirituality

A feeling of emptiness is common among lonely people. One possible explanation is that they have lost contact with their own spirituality, that vitality that goes beyond the everyday world. We may talk about a relationship with God, or with a Higher Force, or with the Spirit — how we name our spiritual connection is not relevant, but whether or not we feel its energy certainly is.

Feeling the flow of what I will refer to as the Spirit can keep us from feeling all alone in the world: it gives us a sense of being part of something much bigger than ourselves, and that is humbling. While it is important to work on our selves, to understand our selves better and express our selves more truly, we see all this in the context of an unfolding, the Spirit flowing through us to reveal who we are.

Attending to our spiritual life involves some transcendence: it requires us to look beyond the usual physical boundaries, and to move into a realm that is at once solitary and all-encompassing.

Some use prayer to tune in to the Spirit, others use mindfulness and meditation to become aware of a Higher Force that moves within and about us, others again see it in nature in which they take great delight and which they hold in some awe. How we choose to enrich our spiritual life is an individual matter, but attending to this aspect of our life will ensure a great relief from feelings of separation, loneliness and isolation.

LIFE CHOICES
Making a decision
Where does most of our day go? If we categorise very broadly we would find that most of us spend some time of our day at our place of work, and some at home, some with other people — whether work colleagues or family or friends — and some alone.

Some of us are very aware of life minute-to-minute; all available energy goes into the present moment whether alone or with others, whether at work or at play. Most of us, however, are not so aware. We either plunge blindly ahead or else float carelessly about, allowing life to happen to us more often than having much input into the process.

What I am talking about here is different from accepting life and its wonders with delight, with puzzlement, and with curiosity. This requires a basic confidence and faith in the unfolding of life and is rarely accompanied by feelings of loneliness. Rather, those who choose a more solitary existence are more likely to follow this particular path.

To plunge blindly or to float carelessly, however, is to avoid taking responsibility for the direction of our own life. The reason may be fear — the fear of making any true decision about our future. Which path to take of the many? How to be sure of the right decision?

I love this little poem by Judith Rodriguez which emphasises the agony of decision-making. It is called 'How do you know it's the right one?'

> Can you play it on a keyboard?
> On one string?
> Is it partial to silence?
>
> Can you exalt it
> continuously?
> Can you debase it?
>
> Can you look at it curdled
> and pasty
> in the glass after midnight?
>
> And eat it and drink it
> whatever —
> it with its memories
>
> and malaise, years and days of it?
> Must you have it?
> Will you love it or live with it?[12]

So, we diddle and daddle, not sure if this is right or that, until suddenly life happens to us and we wonder what is going on.

Here is Pete talking about this aspect of his life:

I have this tendency to let things happen to me. I suppose I have always been afraid that if I change jobs, for example, the new job will be worse than the old one, and I will have my regrets. The funny thing is that I still have regrets, but it's because other people make things happen and I'm at the receiving end.

When I lost my job six months ago I was devastated, until I realised how much I disliked what I was doing and how alienated I felt with the people in that company. I had become totally shut down and I was behaving like some sort of robot, although when I was away on holiday I would think about what I would really like to be doing instead of this work.

After I was retrenched I fell into this depression that lasted for a while. But then I heard someone interviewed on the radio who had started a business he had always wanted to be involved in, and he talked about how happy he was even though he worked harder than ever and was not making much financially speaking, and I was suddenly inspired. I've just established a small business and I have a couple of people working with me. So far it's going very well, and I have great optimism for it.

With hindsight, I can see that the retrenchment was a push for me — out of the safety of a stable, but tedious and unsatisfying, life. Some days now I'm flying by the seat of my pants, but I would say to anyone 'Go for it! Do what you have to do! Wake up!'

Many of us are like Pete: we feel alienated in our place of work, or where we live, or even within ourselves, but rather than take action we shut down to what is happening to us, as if that will protect us from the reality. But as Pete found, life often has a way of making us sit up and take notice.

For him it was retrenchment, for others it may be a relationship breakdown, or a loss of some other sort. The consequence is usually a chaotic swirl of emotion, with strong feelings of confusion and isolation as we thrash around trying to grab hold of a rudder gone crazy.

Choosing who to be

Over the last few years the world has seen dramatic changes in political and economic systems but I can remember reading somewhere that perhaps historians would realise it was the invention of the TV remote control that was the single most important event of our era. With just the tiniest pressure of a thumb we can change channels and glide over many little worlds of television 'reality', never quite feeling the impact of any one particular message but merely glancing over many.

The channel gliding that the remote control allows us provides an apt analogy: as if, with this bit of technological wizardry in our hands every day, we can skim past choices about how to live, what to believe in, what values to have. Quite simply, we are saturated with possibilities, each of which elicits mixed feelings and opinions. Faced with this multiplicity, how is one to make a clear choice?

It was not long ago that people lived in communities surrounded by others who shared their attitudes and beliefs. Physical distance was the only real barrier. The world might have been a big place but, with the people closest to you living around you and rarely, if ever, challenging your stance, life was safe and relatively simple. Back then, rituals and customs defined what was decided and how it was done. The social organisation assigned a clear role to each person, which helped give them a reason for being.

Now, the cultural landscape has changed drastically. Distances are not barriers to communication — in about twenty-four hours we can see a friend on the other side of the world, and technology has provided communication networks over vaster areas than could have been imagined. An increase in mobility and urbanisation has meant that we are working and living closer to others who have completely different belief systems and cultural traditions.

Socially speaking, we have become involved in many more relationships. We have been urged to listen more carefully to others and to become involved in causes of various kinds. We have been confronted with a variety of potential threats and disasters.

Dr Kenneth J. Gergen, psychologist and author of *The Saturated Self* [13] suggests that we take in many, many little bits of other people's being, their values, their attitudes and their opinions, making them part of how we define our own selves so that we find it more and more difficult to know what we truly believe in.

The healthy, well-adjusted individual, most of us would agree, is an integrated one. The field of psychoanalysis has concerned itself with integration for the sake of mental health.

The irony is that, over the years, schools of therapy have proliferated, and many are based on outrageously different concepts of how the psyche works. The very profession that claims to work at integrating human beings can be quite alarmingly fragmented, with the multiplicity of choices offered becoming more of a problem than those that initially led to therapy.

Even those systems of thought that once provided a core to living — the philosophies and ideologies by which many have lived in the past — are now viewed as merely 'social constructs' of reality. There is no longer one Truth, but many different truths.

So, given all this, how does one define the self? Which, of all the myriad bits of being, are to be taken on board? Where does the self begin and end? Bombarded with possibilities, when does one say 'Enough!' to these possibilities?

The challenge is to develop a much more expansive idea of what this self is. Human beings do not have to revert to the naivety and innocence of past times, or constrict themselves to an integrated ideal that never quite pulls together all the bits.

When we are lonely

Often it is our responses to particular situations and circumstances that tell us most about ourselves. Most of us find it easier to draw conclusions about what is bothering another person, or about the types of people others tend to be, than to understand ourselves.

How do we respond to feelings of loneliness? The answer can be very helpful in revealing our strengths and our weaknesses.

In a study[14] aimed at exploring loneliness, subjects were asked what they did about loneliness when they felt it. Amongst all the responses, four categories emerged.

Of these, the category named 'Sad Passivity' was most strongly related to feelings of great loneliness and most characteristic of younger people. Its responses were crying, sleeping, doing nothing, overeating, taking tranquillisers, watching television and drinking or getting stoned.

The researchers pointed out the similarity between this category and the psychoanalytic concept of 'oral passivity', the attitude of needing to be loved and taken care of, the attempt to 'take in' what one can, to feed an emptiness. And they also pointed out that the hopeless, helpless response was often the result of prolonged loneliness, the type that hangs on in spite of efforts to deal with it.

Other categories were 'Spending Money', a strategy of distraction obviously more common among those financially more secure, and 'Social Contact', involving calling or visiting a friend, and more common among those for whom loneliness is a passing phase only.

The fourth category — 'Active Solitude' — is more an alternative to loneliness, a way of spending time alone in a creative and satisfying way. The responses here included studying, writing, listening to music, exercising, going for a walk, working on a hobby, going to a movie and reading.

The response of any one of us to feelings of loneliness depends very much on how we explain our loneliness: if I feel I have no control over it and that it is because of my own inadequacies, I am likely to feel sad and depressed. If I feel that it is because of external circumstances over which I have no control, I may react with anger and frustration. And if I feel that the causes are controllable and that I can draw on internal resources to deal with it, I am likely to take some sort of positive action — perhaps either making social contact or else devoting my time to active solitude.

How we respond most commonly to loneliness is a guide for us: it can reveal the extent to which we feel in charge of our own lives, or the extent to which we let life just happen. It can reveal our most basic fears about being alone and it can confront us with an attitude that relates not only to loneliness, but to life in general.

It is probable, for example, that those people who respond with sad passivity to feelings of loneliness respond in much the same way to most of life's challenges and difficulties.

Similarly, it is probable that those who respond to feelings of loneliness by replacing it with an alternative — active solitude — will, in general, view life as in their control and potentially rewarding.

BUILDING COMMUNITY
The place of community

Some time ago, one of my children worked on an assignment that involved researching the history of our house and the local area. The house is eighty or so years old and she managed to track down a number of people who had lived in it over the years, including a woman, now in her seventies, who had been born in the front bedroom. Three of her four brothers had also been born there.

'Is the old peppercorn tree still in the back garden?' she asked. 'My brothers and I used to have so much fun in a tree house way up there, looking out onto everyone's yards.'

For days after this contact, there seemed an air of reverence about each of us as we moved through the house, almost as if we were treading a sacred site. The old peppercorn tree, still there, looked older and even wiser than ever it did before and the tumble-down bits and pieces around the place assumed a certain charm. The oldness of the place had somehow been validated.

The enormous gum once standing proud in the middle of the dirt road out front had long since gone, of course, making way for a busy thoroughfare. On those long, hot weekend afternoons, the local kids would scramble up into its branches and look out for the odd car to pass by. Or they'd go roller-skating up the road at the local community hall, now a thriving suburban theatre.

'It was a real little community then,' remarked one old woman who'd grown up just around the corner. 'We all knew each other, and everyone cared.'

It's words like these that prompt nostalgia. Distorted our perceptions of days gone may be, and perhaps the hardships of those days have been firmly repressed by these charming people who recount only stories of fun and mischief — of the milkman's cart and the scrumptious bread you bought for a penny from the old stone bakery up the road.

But all the same, there is this yearning for how things used to be, a longing for the simplicity and closeness, a hunger for the blessings of what the old lady called 'a real little community'. It seems that community may have been easier to achieve back then than it is now.

In *The Different Drum*, Dr M. Scott Peck examines the notion of community and its dynamics. 'In and through community lies the salvation of the world. Nothing is more important. Yet ... most of us have never had an experience of true community.'[15]

This is a sad comment on a world that prides itself on advanced and sophisticated methods of communication. But the technological surge forward, with its emphasis on the mechanistic, the competitive and the race for power, has left in its wake the fragmentation and emotional isolation of human beings. The nurturing and support, the comfort and safety that real community can provide have been overlooked, yet they are the very things necessary for the true advancement of the human race and the buoyancy of the human spirit.

Crisis will often precipitate a type of community. A spate of robberies in our street brought a number of us into close contact with each other, sharing the sense of violation, the loss, the fears of recurrence and the frustration and sadness engendered by what was seen to be a symptom of an ailing society. But before long, things settled down, we all went back to our day-to-day activities, which didn't include communicating with neighbours much at all, and the community spirit, temporarily strong, gradually dissolved.

Where severe crisis, as in war, has brought people together into community, there is evidence of mourning when time comes for the community to disband and members to go their own way. The experience has been so powerful and, on one level, so deeply joyful, that the feelings of grief at its loss are strong.

Characteristics of community

An important characteristic of community is commitment. Members will invariably commit themselves to each other, and at the heart of that, and therefore at the heart of all true community, is acceptance of both individual and cultural differences, with differences celebrated as gifts to be treasured by all members.

When we feel totally accepted and acceptable we feel safe, and members of a true community experience that rare sense of safety in their group. Feeling safe, the defences start peeling away and people become ever more vulnerable. And as they are even more loved and accepted, a real healing process starts to take place.

The paradox is that community is a safe place because its members are healing only after they stop trying to heal each other. We may believe that it is not in our direct power to heal, but it is in our power to accept, and that's where healing really lies.

While it can be a safe place, genuine community is not necessarily without conflict. We use skills in listening and understanding, we recognise each other's gifts and limitations and respect and accept them, and in this atmosphere battles can be gracefully fought and conflicts wisely resolved.

Community can crop up in any number of ways in various places. For example, Trish, a woman who describes herself as 'on a voyage of discovery', meets regularly with a group of other women to work on folk-art projects.

It started when I was in the States and enjoyed a little group I met with there. Coming back, I started this little group, and it's been a most wonderful experience.

Mind you, things have not always run smoothly. There have been tensions at different times between different people, but we decided early on that we would help each other learn to be more effective individuals — sometimes things got a bit hot, I can tell you, especially when one person in the group expressed herself rather too frankly. She opened a hornet's nest!

We sit there, working away, chatting and laughing, and then sometimes something will come up — a problem someone is having at home, let's say, and the others listen and give words of support, and usually someone will come up with a new way of seeing things which helps.

I think it's the best sort of community you could have. It's just seven of us, but we've come to care for each other very deeply.

Being together with others and having some common purpose — which may simply be to enjoy each other's company — is a soul-nourishing experience. When we can express ourselves amongst others who can do the same, and when we can share our lives with laughter and understanding, then we can feel truly embraced. When we are part of a community of this sort we can feel we have returned to the bosom of our family, which — if we look beyond the narrow concept of family — is just what we have done.

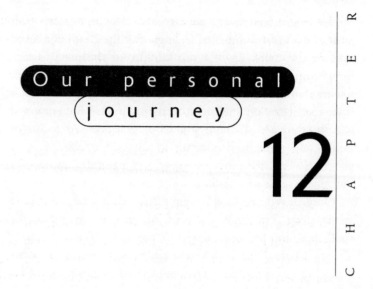

THE PAIN OF LONELINESS
Inner loss, outer loss

There are times in our lives when the pain of loneliness is most acutely felt. There may be loss involved — the loss of a close relationship, the loss of simple companionship, of security, of a future as we had planned it to be, or even of the duties and responsibilities which, although they seemed tiresome at the time, gave us some meaning in our lives.

Any loss will trigger a range of feelings, which is healthy and perfectly natural. Interestingly, despite the emphasis over the last few years on the importance of recognising, acknowledging and managing feelings, there is still a great deal of resistance to effectively dealing with them. There is suspicion surrounding those who are outspoken about how they feel, and while emotional honesty and openness can provide a convenient excuse for self-indulgence for a few, we need to keep in mind that respect for, and attention to, our emotional lives is not only an attainable goal, but a necessary one.

We might feel anger, sadness, rage, despair, anxiety, guilt or any of a great number of feelings after the death of a loved one, or the break-up of a relationship, or the need to face unwelcome and difficult change in life. The feelings might rise in a confused bundle so that we can hardly know what it is we feel at any one moment, so tightly bound and entwined and knotted are all those strands of emotion. At a loss to understand what is happening to us, and unable to cope effectively, we are often intensely and painfully aware of a staggering sense of isolation.

Outer loss is mirrored by inner loss, although this is a more subtle story. The inner sense of loss may be related to the soul's yearning for something it may not yet be able to name, a way of being that is desirable but foreign, a need to draw back or away from the current pattern of living in the world and to take a brave leap into that vast unknown space. The intensity of loneliness we experience when we need to move on from a way of being, in a sense leaving the familiar behind, is no less than with those more obvious outer losses.

Loneliness can make us feel burdened by helplessness and hopelessness, by a sense of failure and worthlessness. It can lead to deep feelings of depression that seem impossible to shake off. The pain of loneliness is very real: some of us know that it can be as debilitating as any physical illness.

Much of the pain of loneliness, however, has to do with our fear of it: this also applies to physical illness, in that the more fearful we are of the pain involved the more acutely we feel it. Pain alerts us to the possibility that there is something awry, but we need not always be alarmed by it if it is bearable. In his book *A World Waiting To Be Born*, M. Scott Peck tells us that, as a doctor, he hates unnecessary pain, but, he writes, 'we shall continue to suffer it egregiously until we learn to distinguish far more clearly between that pain which is indeed needless and that which is essential for our healing'.[1]

The aspect of the pain of loneliness that could be described as 'needless' is the anxiety and shame associated with it: as we discussed in Chapter Two, it is loneliness anxiety that motivates a frenzy of activity, and it is loneliness anxiety that claws at us, insisting that we must at all costs avoid being friendless, or even simply alone.

Words of comfort for the sick or the impoverished or the deserted sound trite: all the same, even those in the very depths of loneliness can be reminded that there are others who do not feel lonely in a similar situation. And there are those who are healthy, wealthy, and privileged in many other ways, who also feel intensely lonely.

We should seek help when the pain of loneliness is too great. If we use painkillers — in the form of either drugs and alcohol, or strong defence mechanisms that further isolate us — we neglect a serious condition. Anaesthetics of most types have their place, but it is very limited.

What pain 'is essential for our healing', as Peck put it? The sort that tells us that something has to change. It may be our attitudes or our beliefs, it may be our lifestyle. It may be that we are moving through a time of change and the pain we are feeling is a natural by-product of that. This little poem by W. H. Auden expresses our resistance beautifully:

We would rather be ruined than changed.
We would rather die in our dread
than climb the cross of the moment and
let our illusions die.[2]

The image of 'climb[ing] the cross of the moment' is so accurate: our fear of pain is so intense that sometimes we will do anything to avoid it. Peck has pointed out in an earlier book[3] that 'life is difficult', and it is our resistance to acknowledging that fact that makes it so difficult: if we accepted that it is difficult to begin with, then paradoxically we would find it easier.

When I am finding life difficult, one of the things I am most likely to do is to turn to books that are of an exploratory nature. One book that I discovered during such a time is

The Hero Within[4] by Carol Pearson, and in it she explores, in the Jungian tradition, several archetypes we live by. Amongst these archetypes is 'The Wanderer', who represents those who set out to confront the unknown and to discover who they are. The call to do so surfaces as a yearning in us for our lives to be more satisfying, or as a yearning for a sense of belonging rather than alienation and isolation.

When the time comes for the journey, these Wanderers feel their aloneness, whatever their personal situation: whether they have partners or not, whether or not they have children and friends or have a prestigious job: There is no way to avoid this experience. While some set off on the quest with a great feeling of adventure, others experience it as thrust upon them by a particular life event — usually a devastating one — and feelings of alienation.

At this stage true intimacy is not possible for these people because they are in the process of confronting and dealing with their own aloneness which is necessary to their development as full human beings. However, if Wanderers never commit to the journey they remain aimless wanderers, searching, searching, but never quite finding what it is they seek; if, on the other hand, they commit to the journey — that is, they commit to the search for meaning — they become Seekers, searching for authenticity in themselves and all around them. Ultimately Seekers are looking for the sacred in their lives.

This exploration of the Wanderer and Seeker archetypes was very meaningful to me: I liked it because it helped put my own feelings of loneliness and my sense of being adrift and alone into a perspective that spoke to me. It helped change my perception of what was happening, from being helpless in a situation to taking charge in some way: the idea that a quest had been thrust upon me was quite thrilling.

Loneliness and creativity

Many highly creative individuals recognise the need to be immersed in their own creative process and the consequent depth of loneliness. Out of the scorching fires of their lonely times emerge great works of art — music, paintings, sculptures, literature — that are expressions of the full spectrum of human emotion and experience.

The novelist Thomas Wolfe wrote of the loneliness of creativity: 'Hideous doubt, despair, and dark confusion of the soul a lonely man must know, for he is united to no image save that which he creates himself ... The huge, dark wall of loneliness is around him now ... he cannot escape.'[5]

Herman Hesse, in *Rosshalde*, wrote of another aspect of the creative life. Here, the painter Veraguth, an individual of 'damaged humanity', took up his brush and 'knew nothing of weakness and fear, of suffering, guilt, and failure in life. Neither joyful nor sad, wholly absorbed by his work, he breathed the cold air of creative loneliness, desiring nothing of a world he had forgotten.'[6]

Creative artists we may not be, but during our lifetime we may experience something of what both Wolfe and Hesse wrote about. The emergence of a new self, the phoenix rising from the ashes, can require just as much creativity, and cause as much chaos and despair. In taking our personal journey, in assuming a commitment to personal growth, we are engaging in a giant task of creativity: like those who are honoured for their creative endeavours, we also involve ourselves in the creative process. And as it is for them, it is for us: loneliness is an integral part of the process.

REACHING OUT
Learning empathy

In her autobiography, *Blackberry Winter: My Earlier Years*,[7] Margaret Mead talked of how, having been excluded from sorority life at college, she learnt what it meant both to exclude and to be excluded. It gave her empathy, she wrote, for those people who felt excluded and lonely.

We may learn many things in our lives, but those things that are seared on the soul, the ones that have been most painful for us, provide us with a source of sensitivity and a greater sense of others' fragility. They allow us to understand and to enter another person's experience without intruding, because we feel their pain with them. In Tagore's words: 'There is rain in your soul, my friend, and I have no umbrella. But let me walk beside you for a while.'[8]

To know loneliness ourselves is to know the anguish it can hold: 'If there is one thing I did learn after living on my own in a strange country for a year, it was that many people feel lonely, and feeling so lonely myself at times opened my eyes to how dark it can be.' This is Helen talking, a young woman recently returned from some time overseas.

> Feeling lonely didn't come as a complete surprise — lots of people warned me that it would happen, especially since I hardly knew anyone there when I arrived. At first I was lost in it, miserable and depressed, but it isn't in my nature to brood too much, so I decided to take steps. I got out, met people, read a lot, got to know the place and its history. Before long I was feeling more positive although I still experienced the odd bout of feeling lonely.
>
> I am much more confident in myself — being alone is a welcome break for me these days — but I am aware of all the sadness out there, the feelings of isolation in people who find it hard to know just what to do about it.
>
> These days, after my own experience, I reach out to people much more in a more human-to-human way rather than just a more superficial social way. I listen more than I ever did before.
>
> I feel fortunate to be quite outgoing, although that is not always the great protection against loneliness that some people think. Sometimes you just have to accept the loneliness and move on anyway.

Helen's words are reflected in Rilke's: 'Love your solitude and bear the pain which it has caused you ... be glad of your growing, into which you can take no one else with you, and be good to those who remain behind.'[9]

Teaching the children

As parents and teachers — in the loosest sense of the terms — we have a responsibility to train our young in the capacity to be alone and to revel in their solitude. We need to teach them, too, that loneliness is not to be feared: it is a feeling that most of us experience at some time and to avoid its sting is to avoid facing up to life altogether. This is the case for all 'negative' emotions: there is a strong cultural bias against experiencing them and the drive to find the ultimate panacea for them.

To teach children that life has its joys as well as its pains is to teach them balance, and that is to inspire poise in them: the ability to respond with dignity to life's difficulties, including occasional feelings of isolation and loneliness.

In this hurried, harried life, we need to take time with children to share each day's wonders, but we also need to distance ourselves sometimes, to detach enough to allow them to grow out of our shadow. While parents' lack of involvement and their abandonment are tragedies for children, over-involvement and intrusion can stifle the growth of the self to the extent that the grown child suffers from the early centring of all available energies and feels the lack of it most acutely now.

To remind us of how essential solitude is, psychotherapist Peter Suedfeld tells us that aloneness 'fills a need, removes a lack, impels growth'. The result is that we feel freed from distractions, and 'from the usual restrictions imposed by social norms and the need to maintain face, and the benefits of reducing external stimulation to the point where the still, small internal voices can be heard'.[10]

We must teach our children that to discover one's own true self is a real voyage, as adventurous and exciting and dangerous as any in their favourite storybooks. We can tell them that while their inner self is being fed — with books, and nature, and quiet time — they have no fear of 'remaining stagnant'.

We can show them that we can enjoy being alone and we can enjoy being with others. We can show them that it is no more selfish to take time for ourselves than it is to take time for everyone else.

Our friendships

Perhaps we have had to wrestle with the question of 'What makes a good friend' because we have been disappointed by others, or because we wonder at our own capacity to be a good friend. Like all relationships, friendship requires effort, loyalty and commitment.

For Laura, a woman who has two or three very close friends, 'friendship means you keep in touch no matter how busy you are. I tell my friends just about everything that happens that is meaningful to me, and they do the same. When things have been hard, they've been loving and supportive, and I am grateful to them. I've told them on occasion how much they mean to me.'

In general, women find it easier to engage in this sort of mutually supportive friendship, although not all choose to. However, men can also know the joys of real friendship, even though they may not necessarily share deep secrets of the heart in the same way.

While Laura puts much effort into her friendships, not everyone is willing to. And there are some who would envy Laura so many good friends — for example Don, an older man who admits to 'quite liking' a few colleagues and a couple of his wife's friends, but feels generally disappointed. He says:

> There are probably only half a dozen people who would fit my idea of someone I could enjoy as a friend in the whole country, so what hope do I have of coming across them? I am looking for someone I can talk to on an

intellectual level, someone who sees life the way I do and enjoys the same sorts of things. Sometimes I tell myself that I would rather put up with feeling lonely than put up with some of the people out there in the world. I know I must sound like a snob, but I really can't be bothered wasting my time. I would rather be on my own.

There are many people who would sympathise with what Don has to say about friendship. Their expectations have not been met in the past, and their response flies in the face of the cultural expectation that we must have friends to be happy.

Don's words remind me of those from Arthur Miller's *The Misfits*: 'If I'm gonna be alone I'd rather be by myself.' It is a decision to be respected, although Don says that when he watches his wife interacting with other people and enjoying it he does feel isolated, not because of her involvement, but because he feels that he is 'unable to reach out to others in the way that she can'.

Laura's relationship with her close friends represents one sort: she is close to each of them and shares a good deal with them. But friends do not have to fulfil each of our needs. One friend may be good to have coffee with and to talk over things, and another friend may be just the right person to go on a long hike with. We might spend an entire week away with another, while yet another is someone we can work with on projects. To recognise the different ways friends fit into our lives — and we into theirs — is to acknowledge all our various strengths.

I like these words from *Loneliness* by Irma Kurtz: 'Making of oneself a friend for friends to discover entails making of oneself a person with something to share other than loneliness ... How do we find our interests? In conference with ourselves.'[11]

Here again we come back to the value of solitude and contemplation in our lives. Finally, to be a good friend we must show ourselves friendly, as the old saying goes, but we must also show ourselves to be interesting people. This doesn't mean a superficial show of talents and interests, but rather a willingness to reach out, when it is appropriate, from a strong and secure home base.

COMING HOME TO OURSELVES
Satisfying the soul

In a most delightful story called 'Sealskin, Soulskin' and recounted by Jungian analyst and storyteller Clarissa Pinkola Estés,[12] a woman's sealskin — representing her soul — is stolen by a deeply lonely man who promises to return it to her if only she will stay with him for seven summers. The lonely man represents the ego, that part of us that is engaged with the outer world, of tasks and duties and material gatherings.

Gradually the seal woman's flesh begins to flake, then it cracks and she begins to wither away altogether until the child of the relationship, roused by a sound he cannot recognise, stumbles across the pelt and, with both joy and grief in his heart, returns it to his mother, knowing that his find will mean his mother's leaving.

> It is the child who brings the sealskin, soulskin back to his mother. It is the child who enables her to return to her home. This child is a spiritual power that impels us to continue our important work, to push back, change our lives, better the community, join in helping to balance the world ... all by returning to home. If one wants to participate in these things, the difficult marriage between soul and ego must be made, the spirit child must be brought to life. Retrieval and return are the goals for mastery.[13]

There are similar stories in various cultures, and sometimes it is the lonely woman who steals from the male. The gender of each is irrelevant here, but the essence of the story clearly tells of the process familiar to many of us: the eventual withering away of the soul when we focus on the externals of the world, trying to engage our reluctant soul along the way.

The man in the story thought that by stealing the sealskin — the soul — he would relieve his loneliness. Instead, he intensified it because the soul knows, finally, what it needs and wants.

The child who regularly visits the sea to converse with the seal woman tells us about the need for solitude in our lives. 'Solitude,' Estés writes, 'is not an absence of energy or action … but is rather a boon of wild provisions transmitted to us from the soul.'[14] The ancients used it as a preventative measure and to heal fatigue, as well as using it to listen to the inner self 'to solicit advice and guidance otherwise impossible to hear in the din of daily life'. Learn the skill of internal solitude, she tells us. Learn to tune out when you are in a room full of people. Turn inward for your much-needed solitude if it is not possible to remove yourself entirely.

This is one of my favourite stories: the image of the seal whose pelt is stolen is poignant, and the pull between parts of ourselves — our ego and our soul in this case — tells a common tale. The story points to the fact that, whatever our lonely self promises if only we will relieve it, we must be clear about what we need to nourish ourselves. It tells us, too, that what the ego calls 'loneliness' the soul calls 'solitude'.

Our view of life

Years ago, when I spent a weekend at a workshop[15] on using the art of aikido as a metaphor for conflict resolution, I saw for myself the power in moving from 'a point of view to a viewing point'.

When we look at life from our own point of view our vision is necessarily limited: in aikido terms, I am confronted with another individual who holds a different point of view, and we stand face to face. However, what if I swing myself gently around and surprise the other by standing there beside them, looking out not only at their view, but at my own view and that of others as well? In choosing to move to this viewing point, I have chosen to expand my view and expand my range of responses too.

Loneliness is often a consequence of unmet expectations and of very particular perceptions. If I spend time thinking about what others should be doing, and how they have let me down, and how they could be doing things much better than they are, it is likely that I suffer from not having my expectations met. And, if I see myself and others in a particular light, if I view being alone, for example, as an aversive experience, then I have perceptions of the world and its people, including myself, that are not working well for me.

I have always liked the sense of the word 'surrender'. It has a serene quality for me, although I do recognise that this is my own perception of the word: others may feel that it hints at weakness and failure, especially in the context of war. But I do feel there is great peace in surrendering: for the lonely person, it is worth considering what could be surrendered. An expectation? A point of view? A preoccupation with self? A preoccupation with others? The anxiety of feeling lonely?

I am talking here about surrendering what is intensifying our sense of loneliness and isolation.

Surrender to ourselves

Carl Jung wrote that '... new meaning for life is so often found in the inferior and undeveloped side of the personality'.[16] Through our life experience we come to recognise, if we are fully awake, that we have our very own 'shadow' — a Jungian term for those aspects of ourselves that we have long kept hidden and unrevealed.

Often it is other people who give us all the clues: when we find we are in conflict with someone else, or when someone's behaviour irritates us, we can usually, if we look hard enough, find something there about ourselves that we have preferred to keep submerged in the subconscious.

In coming to terms with our own shadow we come to terms with others'. How could we not? When we acknowledge our own frailties, unless self-righteousness is one of those we refuse to admit to, it is difficult not to feel more compassionate about the frailties of other people. We hide our shadow side for good reason, after all: every one of us wants, at heart, to be loved, admired and respected.

Coming to like ourselves may be a gradual process. Poet Jim Provencher says it like this in his poem 'Birthday & Us':

But 40
takes 2 years
getting used to
the beginning
of some kind of
inner truce
some final kind
of personal acceptance

frets & worries still
come and go
as pesky flies
with the seasons
some kindness
toward self
gradually grows
if you let it ...[17]

In learning to like and accept ourselves, we can face our loneliness more squarely. Am I too afraid of what others think? we might ask ourselves. Am I so afraid to be alone that I am needy of other people, and they retreat in self-defence? Do I feel dull and boring, stupid and selfish, so that no-one would be interested in befriending me? Do I feel that no-one understands me, and that people wouldn't like me if they knew some of my shameful thoughts?

These are the sorts of questions lonely people ask themselves every day: the choice is to keep asking them or to take some action. If the choice is action, the first step is to accept that we feel very lonely.

In accepting our loneliness, we need to practise being alone and feeling comfortable with that, before aiming to establish a solid base of casual friendships. Sometimes it is the internal pressure to find someone with whom to be intimate that makes us feel lonelier than ever. Casual friendships are a good place to start: we can practise liking who we are around them, before opening up more and more to a casual friend whom we can most trust.

As we saw earlier, self-disclosure is sometimes used as a marketable commodity: because to be friendly is thought to entail being open and honest, sometimes people will tell too much in a bid to win friendship and intimacy. But most of us are frightened off by too much self-disclosure too early. If you are intending to approach a casual friendship with some open, from-the-heart communication, take heed.

While there is no doubt that other people in our lives can provide us with comfort and companionship and fun and meaning, finally we must take responsibility for our own happiness. As one writer says, 'like the fabled musk deer that wanders the forest, searching for the source of the beautiful odour and not realising the scent comes from itself, we often seem to be looking in the wrong place for our happiness and sense of self-worth'.[18]

Embracing loneliness

Once we truly embrace loneliness as a part of our lives, we can engage in a renewed awareness of ourselves. If we regard it as Emily Dickinson did, as 'the Maker of the soul', then we might actually revel in the experience.

If life is a spiritual pilgrimage, it makes sense that loneliness is a part of it since we each have our own individual journey to undertake: it is up to us whether or not we allow our loneliness to help illuminate our path. Retreat from the world is usually necessary to help us sort out where we are headed, and times of loneliness can be used to reflect deeply, to sharpen our perception and to practise insight.

When loneliness is unbearable it is essential to seek help: chronically lonely people have a tendency to blame themselves for feeling as they do rather than acknowledging the impact of situational factors. Blaming ourselves undermines our self-esteem and self-concept and so an endless cycle may be put in motion: feeling bad about ourselves we either avoid other people or seek them out in wild desperation, but both approaches only serve to exacerbate the loneliness. Recognising that loneliness is widely experienced can help us to feel less isolated but further help may be needed to change any self-defeating behaviour patterns that are keeping us locked into lonely feelings.

Recognising the role that our cultural mores play can also help: once we can move from the socially accepted beliefs that urge us to be coupled and to engage in a good deal of social activity in order to keep loneliness at bay, then we may be able to perceive our state in a new way. It takes courage to detach from social standards and to decide for ourselves what works best for us regardless of what others believe. Some solitary time can help us reach a position of equilibrium where we can make such decisions.

Henry David Thoreau recognised the pleasures of solitude. 'I am no more lonely,' he wrote during the extensive time on his own, 'than a single mullein or dandelion in a pasture, or a bean leaf, or sorrel, or a horsefly, or a humble-bee.'[19] Here was an individual who rejoiced in his fundamental relationship with all of life. Consequently he led a life of solitude and creativity rather than loneliness and despair.

The writings of Thoreau and others are an inspiration to those of us for whom being alone for any length of time is a potentially threatening experience. They provide personal evidence that solitude in itself does not inevitably result in

loneliness and that, for those who are alone, a shift in language from 'a lonely life' to 'a solitary life' can mean a shift in perception and a corresponding sense of renewal.

Notes

Chapter one

1 Mijuskovic, B. L. (1979) *Loneliness in Philosophy, Psychology and Literature*. Assen, Netherlands: Van Gorcum.

2 Zilboorg, G. (January, 1938) 'Loneliness'. *Atlantic Monthly,* pp. 45–54.

3 Weiss, R. S. (1973) *Loneliness: The Experience of Emotional and Social Isolation.* Cambridge, MA: MIT Press. The study of loneliness was, at the time of this publication, in its infancy, and the work of Weiss has been regarded as a significant contribution to the development of the subject.

4 Fromm-Reichmann, F. 'Loneliness'. *Psychiatry,* 1959, 22, pp. 1–15.

5 Weiss, R. S. op. cit., p. 15.

6 Carroll, L. (1973) *Alice's Adventures in Wonderland and Through the Looking glass.* London: Dent.

7 Twain, M. *The Adventures of Huckleberry Finn.* New York: Harper and Row.

8 Salinger, J. D. (1951) *The Catcher in the Rye.* London: The Penguin Group.

9 Keats, J. (1818–19) 'Hyperion. A Fragment'. In *The Poems of John Keats,* edited by M. Allott. London: Longman Group Ltd.

10 Coleridge, S. T. 'The Rime of the Ancient Mariner'. In *The Norton Anthology of Poetry.* Third edition. (1983) New York; London: W.W. Norton & Co., Inc.

11 Gordon, S. (1976) *Lonely in America.* New York: Simon and Schuster, p. 26.

12 Sullivan, H. S. (1953) *The Interpersonal Theory of Psychiatry.* New York: Norton, p. 290.

13 Weiss, R. S. op. cit., p. 17.

14 Sermat, V. (1978) 'Sources of Loneliness'. *Essence,* 2 (4), p. 274.

15 Weiss, R. S. (1989) 'Reflections on the Present State of Loneliness Research'. In M. Hojat and R. Crandall (eds), *Loneliness: Theory,*

Research and Applications. A special issue of the *Journal of Social Behaviour and Personality,* p. 8.

16 Gordon, S. op. cit., p. 16.

17 Levy, R. I. (1973) *Tahitians: Mind and Experience in the Society Islands.* Chicago: University of Chicago Press, p. 306.

18 Roberts, C., Davies, E. & Jupp, R. (1992) *Language and Discrimination,* Longman Group, U.K. Ltd, p. 67.

19 Research by Kleck, K. E. et al. (1966) cited in D. Perlman and P. Joshi (1989) 'The Revelation of Loneliness'. In M. Hojat and R. Crandall (eds), p. 66.

20 Fromm-Reichmann, F., op cit., p. 64.

21 Research by Borys, S. & Perlman, D. (1985) cited in D. Perlman and P. Joshi (1989) 'The Revelation of Loneliness'. In M. Hojat and R. Crandall (eds), p. 68.

22 Research by Cozby, P. C. (1973) cited in Hojat and Crandall (eds), p. 68.

23 Research by Russell, D., Peplau, L. A. & Cutrona, C. E. (1980) cited in Hojat and Crandall (eds), p. 68.

24 Wintrob, H. L. (1989) 'Self Disclosure as a Marketable Commodity'. In M. Hojat and R. Crandall (eds), pp. 77–88.

25 ibid.

Chapter two

1 Zilboorg, G. (1938) 'Loneliness'. *Atlantic Monthly,* pp. 45–54.

2 Sullivan, H. S. (1953) *The Interpersonal Theory of Psychiatry.* New York: Norton.

3 Fromm-Reichmann, F. (1959) 'Loneliness'. *Psychiatry,* 22, pp. 1–15.

4 Rogers, C. (1973) 'The Lonely Person — and His Experiences in an Encounter Group'. In *Carl Rogers on Encounter Groups.* New York: Harper & Row, p. 119.

5 ibid., p. 121.

6 Riesman, D., Glazer, N. & Denney, R. (1961) *The Lonely Crowd: A Study of the Changing American Character.* New Haven: Yale University Press.

7   Slater, P. (1976) *The Pursuit of Loneliness*. Boston: Beacon Press, p. 34.

8   Moustakas, C. (1972) *Loneliness and Love*. Englewood Cliffs, NJ: Prentice-Hall.

9   ibid., p. 20. Reprinted by permission of the publisher, Prentice Hall Press/a Division of Simon & Schuster.

10   ibid., p. 21.

11   Mijuskovic, B.L. (1979) *Loneliness in Philosophy, Psychology and Literature*. Assen: Van Gorcum Publishers, p. 49.

12   Weiss, R. S. (1973) *Loneliness: The Experience of Emotional and Social Isolation*. Cambridge, MA: MIT Press.

13   ibid., p. 18.

14   ibid., p. 19.

15   de Jong-Gierveld, J. & Raadschelder, J. (1982) 'Types of Loneliness'. In L. A. Peplau and D. Perlman (eds), *Loneliness: A Sourcebook of Current Theory, Research and Therapy*. New York: John Wiley & Sons, pp. 105–119.

16   Horowitz, L. M., de S. French, R. & Anderson, C. A. (1982) 'The Prototype of a Lonely Person'. In L. A. Peplau and D. Perlman (eds), pp. 183–205.

17   de Jong-Gierveld, J. & Raadschelders, J. (1982) 'Types of Loneliness'. In L. A. Peplau and D. Perlman (eds), pp. 105–119.

Chapter three

1   Jung, C. G. (1966) *Collected Works*, Vol. VII, Sir H. Read, M. Fordham, G. Adler & W. McGuire, trans. by R. F. C. Hull. London: Routledge and Kegan Paul, p. 238.

2   Cooley, C. (1902) *Human Nature and Social Order*, New York: Shocken Books.

3   Cutrona, C. E. (1982) 'Transition to College: Loneliness and the process of social adjustment'. In L. A. Peplau and D. Perlman (eds) *Loneliness: A Sourcebook of Current Theory, Research and Therapy*. New York: John Wiley & Sons, pp. 291–309.

4   James, W. (1908) *Psychology*. New York: Henry Holt, p. 187.

5 Research by Parmelee, P. & Werner, C. (1978) cited in L. A. Peplau
   and D. Perlman (eds), p. 146. More recently, a study by K. Rotenberg
   and J. Kmill in 1992 and involving 275 undergraduates revealed that
   people are less accepting of lonely individuals than the non-lonely.

6 Larson, R., Csikszentmihalyi, M. & Graef, R. (1982) 'Time Alone in
   Daily Experience: Loneliness or Renewal?'. In L. A. Peplau and D.
   Perlman (eds), p. 148.

7 Wolfe, T. (1941) *The Hills Beyond*. New York; London: Harper and
   Bros.

8 Schneider, C. D. (1992) *Shame, Privacy and Exposure*. New York:
   Norton.

9 ibid.

10 Young, J. E. (1982) 'Loneliness, Depression and Cognitive Therapy:
   Theory and Application'. In L. A. Peplau and D. Pearlman (eds), p. 403.

Chapter four

1 Bowlby, J. (1969) 'Affectional Bonds: Their Nature and Origin'. In
   R. S. Weiss, *The Experience of Emotional and Social Isolation*.
   Cambridge, MA: MIT Press, p. 40.

2 Weiss, R. S. (1987) 'Reflections on the Present State of Loneliness
   Research'. In M. Hojat and R. Crandall (eds), *Loneliness: Theory,
   Research and Applications*. A special issue of the *Journal of Social
   Behaviour and Personality*, p. 4.

3 For references to these studies, see Shaver, P. & Hazan, C. (1989)
   'Loneliness, love and attachment'. In M. Hojat and R. Crandall (eds),
   Loneliness: Theory, Research and Applications, p. 97.

4 ibid., p. 96.

5 Ainsworth, M. D. S., Blehar, M. C., Waters, E. & Wall, S. (1978)
   Patterns of Attachment. Hillsdale, NJ: Erlbaum.

6 ibid.

7 Research by Lobdell, J. & Perlman, D. (1986) cited in M. Hojat and
   R. Crandall (eds), p. 22.

8 Andersson, L., Mullins, L. C. & Johnson, D. P. (1989) 'Parental
   Intrusion Versus Socialisation: a dichotomous view of the sources of

loneliness', in M. Hojat and R. Crandall (eds). The average age of the participants was 77 years. The researchers involved realised that the experiences they recalled belonged to child-rearing of 70 years ago, and also that they were relying on memories of these elderly folk that may not have been entirely accurate. However, the results point to the need to consider the role of parental intrusion in the development of the child and later experience of loneliness.

9 For research see Shaver, P. & Hazan, C. (1989) 'Loneliness, Love and Attachment'. In M. Hojat and R. Crandall (eds) *Loneliness: Theory, Research and Applications*. A special issue of the *Journal of Social Behaviour and Personality*.

10 ibid.

11 Sullivan, H.S.(1953) *The Interpersonal Theory of Psychiatry*. New York: Norton.

12 Connolly, J. & Doyle, A. (1984) 'Relation of Social Fantasy Play to Social Competence in Preschoolers'. *Developmental Psychology*, 20, pp. 797–806.

13 Jean Piaget, a Swiss psychologist, has focused on developing a theory of cognitive development during the stages of life from infancy to adolescence.

14 Piaget, J. & Inhelder, B. (1969) *The Psychology of the Child*. New York: Basic Books.

15 For example, Gold, D. T. (1987) 'Siblings in Old Age: Something Special'. *Canadian Journal on Aging*, 6, pp. 199–215.

16 Bossard, J. H. S. (1975) *The Large Family System: An Original Study in the Sociology of Family Behaviour*. Westport Conneticut: Greenwood Press.

Chapter five

1 Erikson, E. H. (1950) *Childhood and Society*. New York: Norton.

2 Research by Brennan, T. & Auslander, N. (1978) cited in T. Brennan: 'Loneliness at Adolescence'. In L. A. Peplau and D. Perlman (eds) *Loneliness: A Sourcebook of Current Theory, Research and Therapy*. New York: John Wiley and Sons, p. 271.

3 Research by Ostrov, E. & Offer, D. (1978) cited in T. Brennan, p. 272.

4 Weiss, R. S. (1973) *Loneliness: The Experience of Emotional and Social Isolation*. Cambridge, MA: MIT Press, p. 93.

5 The term 'individuation' was used by Carl Jung to refer to the process of recognition and acceptance of the opposites within us and the eventual realisation that the Self is both individual and universal. The concept of individuation is central to Jung's theories.

6 Research by Brennan, T. & Auslander, N. (1979) cited in T. Brennan, p. 277.

7 Irvine, J. (April, 1994) 'Putting Parenting before Pride', *Sydney News*, p. 9.

Chapter six

1 Erikson, E. (1974) *Dimensions of a New Identity*. New York: Norton, p. 124.

2 Estés, C. P. (1992) *Women Who Run With The Wolves*. London: Rider, p. 181.

3 This is the name of Gerald O'Collins' book subtitled *Spiritual Awareness and the Mid-Life Crisis* (1985). Australia: Dove Communications.

4 Jung, C. G. (1933) *Modern Man in Search of a Soul*, trans. by W. S. Dell & C. F. Baynes. New York: Harcourt, Brace, Jovanovich, p. 108.

5 O'Collins, G., *The Second Journey*, p. 67.

6 From Muggeridge, M. *Jesus Rediscovered*, quoted in Gerald O'Collins, *The Second Journey*, p. 13.

7 Lopata, H. Z., Heinemann, G. D. & Baum, J. (1969) 'Loneliness: Antecedents and Coping Strategies in the Lives of Widows'. In L.A. Peplau and D. Perlman (eds), *Loneliness: A Sourcebook of Current Theory, Research and Therapy*. New York: John Wiley and Sons, pp. 310–326.

8 ibid., p. 324.

9 For example, research by Arling, G. (1976) cited in L. A. Peplau and D. Perlman (eds).

10 Jung, C.G. (1933) *Modern Man in Search of a Soul*, p. 108.

Chapter seven

1 Moustakas, C. (1968) *Individuality and Encounter*. Cambridge, Mass: Howard A. Doyle Publishing Co., p. 20.

2 Sarton, M. (April, 1974) 'The Rewards of a Solitary Life'. In the *New York Times*.

3 Theroux, P. (1979) *The Old Patagonian Express*. Boston: Houghton Mifflin, p. 391.

4 Suedfeld, P. (1982) 'Aloneness as a Healing Experience'. In L.A. Peplau and D. Perlman (eds), *Loneliness: A Sourcebook of Current Theory, Research and Therapy*. New York: John Wiley and Sons, p. 56.

5 Arendt, H. (1978) *The Life of the Mind*. London: Secker and Warburg, p. 185.

6 Briggs, D. C. (1977) *Celebrate Yourself*. New York: Doubleday, p. 143.

7 Research by Larsen, R. et al. (1985) cited in Mullins, L. C., Johnson, D. P. & Andersson, L., 'Loneliness of the Elderly: The Impact of Family and Friends'. In M. Hojat and R. Crandall (eds), *Loneliness: Theory, Research and Applications*. A special issue of the *Journal of Social Behaviour and Personality*, p. 227.

8 Kurtz, I. (1983) *Loneliness*. Oxford: Blackwell Ltd, p. 115.

9 Winnicott, D. (1958) 'The Capacity to be Alone'. *International Journal of Psychoanalysis*, 39, pp. 416–20.

10 Kurtz, I. op cit., p. 74.

11 Rubenstein, C. & Shaver, P. (1982) 'The Experience of Loneliness'. In L.A. Peplau and D. Perlman (eds), *Loneliness. A Sourcebook of Current Theory, Research and Therapy*, p. 221.

12 ibid., p. 221.

13 Anson, P. (1964) *The Call of the Desert — The Solitary Life in the Christian Church*. London: William Clowes and Sons Ltd, p. 1.

14 Byrd, R. E. (1938) *Alone*. New York: Ace.

15 Cottee, K. (1989) *A History-Making Solo Voyage Around the World*. Australia: Macmillan Co., p. 106.

16 Suedfeld, P. (1982) 'Aloneness as a Healing Experience'. In

L.A. Peplau & D. Perlman (eds), *Loneliness: A Sourcebook of Current Theory, Research and Therapy*, p. 65.

Chapter eight

1 Dowrick, S. (1991, first publ.) *Intimacy and Solitude*. Australia: William Heinemann, p. 5.

2 Bowlby, J. (1969) 'Affectional Bonds: Their Nature and Origin'. In R. S. Weiss, *The Experience of Emotional and Social Isolation*. Cambridge, MA: MIT Press, p. 38.

3 Johnson, R. A. (1983) *The Psychology of Romantic Love*. London, Penguin Group, p. xii.

4 ibid., p. xii.

5 Research cited in Shaver, P. & Hazan, C. (1989) *Loneliness, Love and Attachment*. In M. Hojat and R. Crandall (eds), *Loneliness: Theory, Research and Applications*. A special issue of the *Journal of Social Behaviour and Personality*.

6 Peck, M. S. (1978) *The Road Less Travelled*. New York: Simon & Schuster, p. 168.

7 Kurtz, I. (1983) *Loneliness*. Oxford: Blackwell Ltd, p. 102.

8 Research cited in Shaver, P. & Hazan, C. (1989) 'Loneliness, Love and Attachment. In M. Hojat & R. Crandall (eds).

9 Jansen, D. & Newman, M. (1989) *Really Relating*. Century Hutchinson Australia Pty Ltd, p. 201.

10 ibid, p. 201.

11 Lynch, J. (1977) *The Broken Heart*. New York: Basic Books, p. 215.

12 ibid., p. 218.

13 Norwood, R. (1985) *Women Who Love Too Much*. London: Arrow Books Ltd, p. 240.

Chapter nine

1 Burns, R. (1993) *Managing People in Changing Times*. Australia: Allen and Unwin, p. 15.

2 Schwartz, H. S. (1990) *Narcissistic Process and Corporate Decay: The Theory of the Organisation Ideal*. New York: New York University Press.

3 Burns, R. op. cit., p. 77.

4 Llewellyn, K. (1987) *The Waterlily*. Australia: Hudson Publishing, p. 17.

5 Robinson, B. (1989) *Work Addiction*. Deerfield Beach, Florida: Health Communications Inc.

6 For example Konopka, G., (1966) and Stierlin, H. (1974) cited in T. Brennan 'Loneliness at Adolescence'. In L. A. Peplau and D. Perlman (eds), *Loneliness: A Sourcebook of Current Theory, Research and Therapy*. New York: John Wiley and Sons, p. 278.

7 Fromm, E. (1941) *Escape from Freedom*. New York: Holt Rinehart.

8 Elias, N. (1991) *The Society of Individuals*. Oxford: Blackwell, pp. 196–7.

9 ibid., p. 198.

10 Hofstede, G. (1980) 'Motivation, Leadership, and Organisation: Do American Theories Apply Abroad?' In *Organisational Dynamics*, pp. 42–63.

Chapter ten

1 Dossey, L. (1991) *Meaning & Medicine*. New York: Bantam Books, p. 91.

2 Bartrop, R., Lazarus, L., Luckhurst, E., Kiloh, L. G. & Penny, R. (1977) 'Depressed Lymphocyte Function After Bereavement'. In *Lancet*, 1, pp. 834–9.

3 Dossey, L. op. cit., p. 90.

4 ibid., pp. 90–1.

5 Bohm, D. quoted in L. Dossey, *Meaning &Medicine*.

6 ibid, p. 101.

7 Research by Berkman, L. & Syme, S. (1982) cited in L. Dossey, *Meaning and Medicine*, p. 94.

8 Rubenstein, C. & Shaver, P. (1982) 'The Experience of Loneliness'. In L. A. Peplau and D. Perlman (eds) *Loneliness: A Sourcebook of Current Theory, Research and Therapy*. New York: John Wiley and Sons, p. 211.

9 Dacher, E. S. (1991) *PNI: The New Mind/Body Healing Program*. New York: Paragon House, p. 34.

10 Borysenko, J. (1987) *Minding the Body, Mending the Mind*. Reading, Mass: Addison-Wesley Publishing Co. Inc., p. 34.

11 Montagu, A. (1971) *Touching: The Human Significance of the Skin*. New York: Harper and Row, p. 290.

12 Burns, R. (1993) *Managing People in Changing Times*. Australia: Allen and Unwin, p. 15.

13 Dacher, E. S., op. cit., p. 134.

Chapter eleven

1 Experimental communities, of which the commune is an example, have been established throughout history and have often attracted those whose values oppose the norms of society. There is usually a strong emphasis on interpersonal relationships, and members need to be comfortable with the process of intimacy since they need not only to be clear about their beliefs and values, but to care about each other as well.

2 In *The Waning of Humaneness*, Konrad Lorenz (Unwin Hyman, 1983) presents a detailed discussion of this topic in a chapter appropriately entitled 'Malfunctions of Once Meaningful Behaviour Patterns'.

3 Montagu, A. (1971) *Touching: The Human Significance of the Skin*. New York: Harper and Row.

4 Most of us have developed a whole range of masks, many of which serve to protect us and are perfectly necessary in certain situations. 'Every profound spirit needs a mask', according to Nietzsche. But too often we become confused about where the mask ends and 'I' begin, and we can fool ourselves that this mask or that one is actually who I am. It takes some careful sensing and contemplation to make the distinction.

5 Forster, E. M. (1910) *Howards End*. London: Hodder and Stoughton, epigraph.

6 Not everyone concurs with this view, believing that the child regards itself as separate all along and has feelings of union only after developing strong senses of self and other.

7 Fromm, E. (1956) 'The Theory of Love' from *The Art of Loving* and reproduced in *Bridges not Walls* (1977), edited by John Stewart. Philippines: Addison-Wesley Publishing Co., Inc., p. 254.

8 Jean-Paul Sartre's term for a Higher Force, or God, is 'Other'.

9 Ornish, D. (1990) *Dr Dean Ornish's Program for Reversing Heart Disease.* New York: Random House, p. 245.

10 Milton, J. 1968 *Paradise Lost.* England: Penguin Books Ltd.

11 Ornish, D. op.cit., p. 245.

12 Rodriguez, J. (1988) 'How do You Know it's the Right One?' from *Judith Rodriguez New and Selected Poems.* Australia: University of Queensland Press, p. 212.

13 Gergen, K. J. (1991) *The Saturated Self.* New York: Basic Books.

14 Rubensten, C. & Shaver, P. (1982) 'The Experience of Loneliness'. In L. A. Peplau and D. Perlman (eds), *Loneliness: A Sourcebook of Current Theory, Research, and Therapy.* New York: John Wiley and Sons, p. 215.

15 Peck, M. S. (1987) *The Different Drum.* New York: Simon & Schuster, p. 17.

Chapter twelve

1 Peck, M. S. (1993) *A World Waiting To Be Born.* A Bantam Book, p. 12.

2 Auden, W. H. (1968) 'The Age of Anxiety' in *Collected Longer Poems. W. H. Auden.* London: Faber & Faber, p. 350.

3 Peck, M. S. (1978) *The Road Less Travelled.* New York: Simon & Schuster, p. 15.

4 Pearson, C. (1989) *The Hero Within.* San Francisco: HarperCollins. The sequel, *Awakening the Heroes Within* (1991), includes various exercises to help us understand how the archetypes work for each of us.

5 Wolfe, T. (1941) *The Hills Beyond.* New York; London: Harper and Bros.

6 Hesse, H. (1986) *Rosshalde.* London: Triad/Grafton, p. 75.

7 Mead, M. (1972) *Blackberry Winter: My Earlier Years.* New York: William Morrow & Co.

8 Tagore, R., quoted in M. d'Apice, *Noon to Nightfall*. (1989) Melbourne: CollinsDove, p. 42.

9 Rilke, R. M. (1954) *Letters to a Young Poet*, trans. Herter Norton. New York: W. W. Norton, p. 37.

10 Suedfeld, P. (1982) 'Aloneness as a Healing Experience'. In L. A. Peplau and D. Perlman (eds), *Loneliness: A Sourcebook of Current Theory, Research and Therapy*. New York: John Wiley and Sons, p. 61.

11 Kurtz, I. (1983) *Loneliness*. Oxford: Blackwell Ltd, p. 11.

12 Estés, C. P. (1992) *Women Who Run With The Wolves*. First publ. in UK by Rider.

13 ibid., p. 273.

14 ibid., p. 293.

15 This was a workshop conducted by aikido master Thomas Crum, author of *The Magic of Conflict*. (1987) New York: Simon & Schuster.

16 Jung, C. G. From *Collected Works, XVII*, and quoted in M. d'Apice, *Noon to Nightfall*. (1989) Melbourne: CollinsDove, p. 50.

17 Provencher, J. (1994) 'Birthday & Us'. In Sue Hicks (ed.) *Five Live*. Sydney: Live Poets' Press, p. 108.

18 Ornish, D. (1990) *Dean Ornish's Program for Reversing Heart Disease*. New York: Random House, p. 96.

19 Thoreau, H. D. (1969) *Walden*. New York: Franklin Watts Inc., p. 147.